TRIALS.
TRIUMPH
&
THE VICTORY

GREGORY AUSTIN GLAUDE

ISBN 978-1-0980-4792-4 (paperback)
ISBN 978-1-0980-4793-1 (digital)

Christian Faith Publishing, Inc.
832 Park Avenue
Meadville, PA 16335
www.christianfaithpublishing.com

Printed in the United States of America

DEDICATION

To my Lord and Savior, Jesus Christ, the Lord of Lords and King of Kings; my parents, William Criss and Phyllis Taylor Glaude; and my wife, Minerva, who I love always and allways, and to anyone who will hear His voice calling them to Eternal Salvation through the words of my testimony. Special thanks to my sister, Kristina, who helped me finalize and edit this book or it would have been a mess!

Thank you,
Gregory Austin Glaude

Contents

PREFACE

To my family, friends, and fellow brothers and sisters in Jesus Christ, please know that the words you are about to read in this book are the words of someone who should be dead. The number of times my life could have been taken is numerous. However, the numbers of times that God has spared my life are even more. This is the testimony of Gregory Austin Glaude, born  November 1, 1958, to Phyllis Taylor Glaude and William Criss Glaude, seen in photo.

"For God so loved the world that He gave His only begotten Son, that whosoever should believe in Him shall not perish but have everlasting life." (John 3:16)

My story is special because it is the testimony that our Lord, Jesus Christ, has given me to tell and so I tell it as often as He permits. As I share my testimony my goal is to do the following:

1. Tell the truth about what has happened in my life and how God has intervened on numerous occasions, literally saving me from death.

2. Encourage those suffering with any type of addiction, sickness, or illness and share the Word of God on how to overcome those problems successfully.

3. Motivate people to believe in the Gospel of our Lord and Savior, Christ Jesus and that you may be baptized and become born again as the Bible says in **John 3:3 (NKJV)**, "Jesus answered and said to him, "Most assuredly, I say to you, *unless one is born again, he cannot see the kingdom of God*" and receive the **FREE GIFT OF SALVATION** because we do not automatically go to Heaven when we die. We must choose Jesus Christ as our Lord and Savior and be baptized for the remission (removal) of our sins.

4. Help others believe in the Saving Power of the Word of God for your physical, emotional, and spiritual healing that you are renewed in mind, body, and spirit.

5. Share this message so others might believe and know there is a *"One True God"* who sent His Son, Jesus Christ, to die for our sins so that we all might be saved eternally.

Have you ever asked yourself, *"Does God really want to heal me or really want to restore me?"*

Jesus Christ desires to heal us both *"physically"* and *"spiritually"* through the Word of God in the Bible. Here are a few Scriptures that show God's willingness to heal us and why I am sharing this book with you:

Jesus Cleanses a Leper (Matthew 8:1–3, NKJV)

[1] When He had come down from the mountain, great multitudes followed Him. [2] And behold, a leper came and worshiped Him, saying, *"Lord, if You are willing, You can make me clean."* [3] Then Jesus put out *His* hand and touched him, saying, *"I am willing; be cleansed."* Immediately his leprosy was cleansed.

A Woman Healed (Matthew 9:20–22, NKJV)

[20] And suddenly, a woman who had a flow of blood for twelve years came from behind and touched the hem of His garment. [21] For she said to herself, *"If only I may touch His garment, I shall be made well."* [22] But Jesus turned around, and when He saw her He said, *"Be of good cheer, daughter; your faith has made you well."* And the woman was made well from that hour.

Jesus Heals A Great Multitude (Matthew 15:30, NKJV)

[30] Then great multitudes came to Him, having with them the lame, blind, mute, maimed, and many others; and they laid them down at Jesus' feet, and He healed them.

Meeting Specific Needs (James 5:13–16, NKJV)

[13] Is anyone among you suffering? Let him pray. Is anyone cheerful? Let him sing psalms. [14] Is anyone among you sick? Let him call for the elders of the church, and let them pray over him, anointing him with oil in the name of the Lord. [15] And the prayer of faith will save the sick, and the Lord will raise him up. And if he has committed sins, he will be forgiven. [16] *Confess your trespasses to one another, and pray for one another, that you may be healed.* The effective, fervent prayer of a righteous man avails much.

Confess Christ Before Men (Matthew 10:32–33, NKJV)

[32] "Therefore whoever confesses Me before men, him I will also confess before My Father who is in heaven. [33] But whoever denies Me before men, him I will also deny before My Father who is in heaven.

Please know that there are so many other instances recorded in the Bible about the *"Healing Power of Jesus Christ."* Just open the New Testament in the Books of Matthew, Mark,

Luke and John and you will see it testifies of His Majesty. My dear friends, the time of God's probation for man to accept Jesus Christ's offer of the Gift of Salvation where all your sins are forgiven is running out. We see every day in the news and in the world that there is evil everywhere. People, especially young people, are dying daily due to murder, abortion, war, and drug overdoses and more. Please take this message seriously.

TRIALS.
TRIUMPH
&
THE VICTORY!
A STORY OF GOD'S SAVING GRACE

This is the testimony of how Gregory Austin Glaude overcame addiction to cigarettes, alcohol, drugs, sin, fought cancer…and SURVIVED and gained a new life in Christ Jesus.

If someone told you, "I know a guy who was hit by a car as a pedestrian and the car was travelling 65mph, had two serious motorcycle accidents, either of them could have been fatal, was held at gunpoint by three guys who wanted to rob him, and finally developed stage four cancer and had four spinal surgeries…and if that weren't enough, also had a TIA or **"mini stroke"** you would think that this person would be dead. The fact is all those things happened to me and this is my story. And yes, I'm still alive so far by God's Grace! The things you are about to read are all true. I know one thing is for certain. God loves me and He's not done with me yet and He wants me to tell you what He's done for me so that you might believe in His awesome love and power to save us all. The things stated above really happened to me and I will share in greater detail later. So let's take a trip back to my earliest memories.

CHAPTER 1

MY EARLIEST MEMORY

 My earliest memory begins at age two and my family was attending a Catholic mass at the Franciscan Monastery in NE Washington, DC, on a Sunday morning. I was in a cotton diaper, no Huggies back then, and in my Sunday best in my mother's arms. My father was on one end of the pew and my older brother, Steve, and older sister, Kristina, were in between Mom and Dad. The church was dark for some reason even though the lights were on, and seemed kind of eerie. Everything was quiet except when there were responses from everyone, otherwise, you could hear the faint voice of the priest. At some point during the service I tried to squirm and say something and my mother pinched me. I looked at her and said, *"You hit me"* (child's translation) and she whispered to me, *"No, I pinched you and I'll do it again if you aren't quiet"* and gave me *"the look."* I immediately complied and here was my first lesson on proper Catholic Church conduct and protocol during church service. Mom did not play that in church. And even though I got a dose of correction there was something special about church and I always seemed to have an attraction to it. I didn't understand the *"mystique"* of church. I just knew you were supposed to always dress nice and sit and be quiet and do what you were told. Stand,

sit, kneel, pray. This was the Catholic way. You were to go to church *"every"* Sunday. No exceptions! That was the call…whether you liked it or not, though it didn't bother me to attend.

When I was six years old, the tradition of church got to be too much for my parents and mom told me one day, *"Even if we don't get up and go to church, I want you to go."* Mom knew the importance of tradition and commitment while raising a *"Good Catholic School"* kid, so the very next Sunday, per mom's request, I got up around 6:30 AM, put on my brown three-piece suit, clip-on tie and matching brown good shoes and I walked to church by myself. I marched all the way to St. Anthony's Church which was about a mile away from our home at 4316 Twelfth Place, NE (see diagram). Rain, snow, or shine I walked to church every Sunday. My sister, Tina, and brother, Steve, also went to church too because back in the day the nuns at St. Martin's Catholic Elementary School, where we attended, would question us on the homily the next day. So right before school started, the kids found the one kid who went to church and ask, *"What was the homily about yesterday?"* And if the nuns asked you, you better have the answer! It was not a good thing to say, *"I don't know…"* Nuns were serious ballers back then. You didn't give them any back-talk! That was a *"no-no"!* It's amazing; by age seven, I had completely memorized the entire church service without reading the booklet handed out each week. The only thing different was the homily. That was the part I

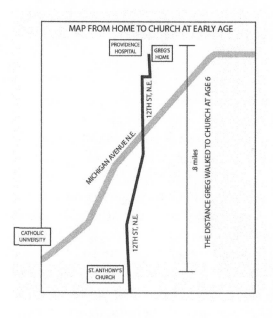

14

liked the most. Things were different in those days. Back then, we used to walk or ride our bicycles everywhere and went outside and *"played real games"* in our backyards, in the alley, the school yard and on the fields of Turkey Thicket, a nearby playground. Parents didn't worry much about their kids getting in trouble, bullied or much less, kidnapped or murdered, when they went outside to play or go to school. It was a safer time and safer environment for the most part, a different time indeed. Now today, children can't walk or don't want to walk two blocks without fear of someone getting hurt, kidnapped or worse. Times have changed.

We lived in Washington, DC, until shortly after my tenth birthday in November of 1968, then, moved to Silver Spring, MD, where my life got flipped upside down. There were a few White people who lived near us in DC and I never really thought much about *"color."* However, after a few months in Silver Spring living in a mostly all White and Jewish neighborhood, I realized that I was *"Not in Kansas anymore or DC for that matter!"* Things were fine at first because I still was going to the same grade school, St. Martins in NE DC until the travel back and forth became too much for mom. So she enrolled me in the nearby parochial school, St. Bernadette's, just a few blocks from home…easy walking distance.

ELEMENTARY SCHOOL: THE ONLY BLACK KID IN SCHOOL

My very first day at St. Bernadette's was quite an experience! Going to a new classroom with all new faces and a new teacher was exciting. However, right from the start there was something very different, I remember standing in the hallway for about fifteen minutes while the principal and teachers for the fifth grade tried to decide *"Which classroom should we put him in?"* You see, there was an "A" and a "B" class for each grade. The "A" classroom was for the "A" class for the good students who excelled in learning… and of course, the "B" class was for the "not so excellent students."

So the teachers gave me the benefit of the doubt and placed me in the "A" class; after all, they didn't want to judge me because of my *"apparent difference,"* even though I looked very much like the other kids. When I walked into the classroom the children burst into applause and I just stood there smiling, having no idea why they were clapping. However, unknown to me, the teacher of the class had announced that they were receiving their *"first black kid"* in their school so they wanted to make me feel welcome! When class resumed, the teacher asked us all to take out pen and paper. Of course, I was empty-handed. However, I never will forget the kindness of one girl, Kathleen, who turned around and offered me a pen and a piece of paper. I really appreciated her kindness. Blending in and being part of the class is really important at any age. Well, the welcome wagon didn't last long though. As soon as we went to recess, I found myself encircled by all the boys of the two fifth grade classes hearing the chants, *"Fight! Fight! Nigger and a White! Fight! Fight! Nigger and a White! Fight! Fight! Nigger and a White!"* For a ten-year-old and my very first day at recess at a brand new school, not knowing anyone, and being sur-rounded by eleven or twelve guys, was pretty frightening to say the least! I had no idea who might jump me from behind or throw a sucker punch. I remember just being in the middle of the circle for what seemed like a lifetime, which was probably only a few min-utes. Before I knew it, one boy got pushed toward me and I tussled with him for a few minutes until one of the girls reported it to one of the nuns (the little ladies who wore the black and white dresses and head bands) who came and broke it up. The incident was not reported to my parents, nor was anything ever said to me in apol-ogy. *"Better just keep things quiet and hope they go away."* That was the Catholic School way. I didn't say anything to my parents about the incident since I managed not to get beat up the first few days. This lasted long enough for the guys to realize that I played base-ball, basketball, and football just as well as any of them. I survived fifth, sixth and seventh grades as they say and lived long enough to go to the eighth grade.

It was 1972 and I was in eighth grade. I remember going to church one Sunday, and ran into my buddy from school, Joe. He and I sat on the side of the church during service and made a few jokes and laughed, but not enough to be noticed…or so we thought. That Monday, during religion class, the priest who offered Sunday Mass came by our classroom and asked Joe and me to stand up and give reason to our behavior in church the day before. Well, of course we didn't have an excuse. What would that sound like? However, while standing there embarrassed, the priest asked *me* to see him in his chambers in the rectory after school. I know some of you may ask the question: Was this priest a pedophile? And to answer your question, *"I don't know!"* The fact is, I didn't go see the priest after school. I had two good reasons…maybe even very good reasons: (1) I was a patrol boy and I had to walk in the line home with the kids that lived in my direction. This was an important responsibility that I had to maintain. (2) This being the most important reason of all. One day our class went into the church for choir practice and this same priest was dressed like a vampire standing in the back of the church. When we walked in, he was facing the front with a huge cape and cowl collar on! One of my friends whispered, *"It's Dracula!"* Well, for an eleven-year-old kid who was deathly afraid of vampires and horror movies, there was absolutely no way I was going to see this priest by myself! NO WAY!

So the next day, the priest showed up at our classroom and said to me, *"You didn't come and see me. Come and see me today."* I replied, *"Okay."* But I had no intentions of showing up to that rectory. I was not going to be bitten by that priest or vampire or whatever he was.

Eighth grade had a lot of turning points for me. Here was where some of the rubber met the road and the face of innocence would be torn away. There was a junior high school down the street from my home and some of the *"bad kids"* that got kicked out of St. B's, ended up there… Eastern Junior High School. I was twelve years old…

I would come home from school, change out of my navy blue uniform pants and my light blue button-down shirt with dark tie into my play clothes, jump on my green Schwinn bicycle and ride down to the school as they were letting out. There was an island in the middle of the road and many of the kids, the *"smokers,"* would stand in groups of twos and threes and light up. As a young kid I used to hate cigarettes, or at least hated seeing young kids smoke. The kids there seemed, as they would say, *"more mature,"* because they were *"emboldened"* to do whatever they wanted, like having sex and smoking. Free from the *"restrictions of Catholic School dogma"* former classmates who left St. B's and attended the public school were not as shy and now more outgoing. Many of the kids would light up a cigarette in front of the school and I used to think, *"No way! I'm not ever doing that!"* When I was thirteen years old, I used to ask kids for cigarettes and then break them in half right in front of them as a protest to their *"evil doings."* I was indeed a *"goodie-two shoes"*! The kids would get upset but we never fought over me breaking the cigarettes. I think in their minds they knew I was right; however, it didn't take long for me to give in to temptation and ignore my *"righteous non-smoking crusade"* before I started smoking.

CHAPTER 2

THE HONDA MINI TRAIL MINI-BIKE

Before we moved to Maryland, if we stayed home from school because we had too much snow, my brother and I would grab the snow shovels and hit the streets shoveling our neighbors' walkways for anywhere from $3–$10 depending on the size of the area that needed clearing. By age seven and eight we had become the entrepreneurs. Well, by the time we moved to Maryland, I carried on the business but now adding lawn-mowing and leaf-raking to my set of skills. I always liked earning money. I didn't have a purpose though…until my buddy Tom back in the old neighborhood got a Honda mini-bike for Christmas. I remember spending the night at his house and his dad took all of us to see it in the dealer's window. There it was, the first little motorcycle I had ever seen for kids. This was no ordinary mini-bike with the lawn-mower engine. This bike looked like a miniature motorcycle with a kick-start and gears and everything! It was just amazing. Well, when summer came around, Tom, Greg, and Tom's brother Ricky came to spend the night and he bought the Honda Mini Trail with him. We took it to the dirt bike trail up the street in the morning and all of us took turns riding. First Tom rode then Greg and then me. I jumped on, took off down the trail and came back up full throttle! I flew past the guys as fast as I could and when I needed to slow down and turn I kept going straight…right into the bushes and trees! I finally stopped and all the guys could do was laugh! I thought Tom would have been upset at me for running into the bushes but he was laughing too hard to worry about the bike. So…we went back to my house, the boys went back home and I started in with a barrage of questions…it was the same one actually, *"Maaa, can I get a Honda Mini-Bike? Maaa, can I get a Honda Mini-Bike? Maaa, can I get a Honda Mini-Bike?"* Well, Mom knew that this wasn't going to go away. So eventually after several weeks of begging and pleading, Mom looked into the cost of a Honda Mini Trail mini-bike but didn't reveal her little secret. However, the cost was too much for her budget.

One day, Mom said to me, *"Let's go for a ride."* It was summer and we went on a ways and I thought to myself, *"Where are we going?"* Then along the way she asked me the question, *"Are you sure you have to have a "Honda Mini-bike? Could you do for another mini-bike?"* And I replied, *"Absolutely not! It has to be a Honda. Nothing else will do."* As we were having the conversation I noticed we were right by Pep Boys. It didn't dawn on me until later that mom was going to buy me a less expensive mini-bike, but I was not having it! My mind was made up. Well it was fall and I was 11 years old and Greg also had a Honda mini-bike and they had just left my house again after a long day in the mini-bike trails. Mom and I were at the front door waving goodbye when I turned and looked at her and said quite upset, *"Maaa! How come I can't get a Honda mini-bike?"*

"Well sweetie, they just cost too much money and I can't afford it."

"Well how much does it cost?"

"Well, they're about $300. I just don't have that kind of money." At age eleven I had no concept of what $300 was or how much it cost to put three children through parochial school, with books and uniforms to boot. But without missing a beat I replied, *"Well, what if I give you half the money?"* Mom was always encouraging but I remember the look she gave me and she, in her mind was processing this; *"He's eleven years old. He doesn't have a job, no income and he doesn't even really have an allowance… Where will he get*

$150?" So mom, in her loving voice said, *"Okay, sweetie, you save your money and we'll see about it."* Well, it was November and the leaves were falling off the tree and it was 6:00 PM and now I was on a mission! I went into the backyard, grabbed Dad's rake and I went to work. I went through my neighborhood raking leaves until 9:30 PM that same evening and came home with $35. *"Maaa! Put this toward my mini-bike!"* At that moment, Mom knew that she had unleashed the work-beast in me and I was on a mission. I was going to get my $150 for my Honda Mini Trail...and soon if I kept it up.

Well, Christmas was approaching and my grandmother would always call to find out what the grandchildren wanted. I remember hearing the conversation mom had with her mother...

"Well, Tina wants her driver's license and Steve wants something or other and Greg wants this thing, a Honda Mini Trail."

"Well, what's that?"

"Well, I have to tell you, it is a miniature motorcycle with all the gadgets on it like a real motorcycle. And I want you to know, he wants it so badly that he's even offered to pay half for it and he's even saved up about $55." Well, my grandmother was very straight forward and believed in rewarding those who worked for it. So she told Mom, *"Well, if any child twelve years old wants something so bad that he is willing to work for it, you tell him I will give him the other half for his mini-bike."* Well, when Mom informed me that Grandmother was going to pay the other half for my dream bike I knew this we in the bag.

In the spring of 1971, Grandmother got ill and was hospitalized and mom would stop by the hospital every day after work. I didn't know why grandmother was there but I told mom to tell her, *"Tell Grandmother I hope she gets well."* Well, Grandma was no fool. She told Mom, *"He doesn't want anything to happen to me because he thinks he won't get that mini-bike if something does."* Well, one summer afternoon I was on the back porch working on my bicycle when I heard mom come in the front door. I looked at her face and there were tears in her eyes and a sadness on her face that I had never seen before. *"Mom, what's wrong?"*

"Your grandmother passed away today." I heard the hurt in her voice and it just wrenched my gut. I had never ever seen my mother cry and I knew she was just devastated and it ate at me to my core. I didn't care about the mini-bike. Grandmother was seemingly so young. I hurt because death had hurt my mom and I couldn't do anything about it. I just started hitting my bicycle with the hammer because I never saw mom cry...about anything. Mom got through her mother's funeral but I knew there was a hurt in her that would never go away.

MY THIRTEENTH BIRTHDAY

Attending Catholic school did have some privileges including special holidays during the year. My birthday always came on a Catholic holiday, All Saints' Day, so every year I got to stay home for my birthday. I remember this particular birthday well. November 1 was to come on a Monday that year and it was Friday afternoon, so I had a long weekend ahead. When mom got home from work that evening, I looked at the car and noticed something different about it...it was sitting low in the back like something really *"heavy"* was sitting in there. Well, I just had to find out. Early Saturday morning, Dad had gotten up about 3:30 AM to go fishing with his buddies. That was his thing. He loved fishing and nothing got him up so early as to prep his coolers and fishing rods and head out to the bay with a group of his friends. So here was my chance to check the trunk and see if I finally got my Honda Mini Trail. All I had to do was to get mom's keys to the car, pop the trunk and pray my dreams were coming true! Mom was in a dead sleep. No problem. However, our dog, Krypto, was sitting right by mom's purse. Now he was my dog basically and he never growled at me, but this morning as I reached for her purse he growled at me like I was doing something wrong and he knew it! GRRRRRRRRRRRR. I knew if he kept it up Mom would have awakened and asked me what I was doing. Three times I tried to reach for the purse but got growled at each time. So I left the room wondering all day long, *"What's in the trunk!?"*

So Sunday morning rolls around and mom called me to the front door and casually said, *"Greg, do me a favor and get the books out of my trunk."*

And I was like, *"Books. Those are books in the trunk?"* Ohhh, the disappointment that flooded my heart just overtook me. So I dragged myself to the car, stuck the key in and popped the trunk open... When the trunk opened all the way I saw the most beautiful candy apple red Honda Mini Trail mini-bike ever! My jaw dropped and I leaped (as Mom would say) ten feet in the air! I jump up and then I looked and realized I couldn't lift the bike out the trunk so I ran inside and mom just had the biggest smile on her face. Dad was at the front door by then and they all saw how excited I was! This was indeed the *"BEST BIRTHDAY PRESENT EVER!"* My dream had come true! And for the record, let me say this; *"HARD WORK DOES PAY OFF!"* It may take a day, a week, a month, a year or sometimes even longer, but if you put your mind to it you can do it. And even better, if you pray and ask God to help. He will lead and direct your paths. I took my victory lap around the neighborhood visiting all my friends showing off my new prize, my pride and joy, my Honda Mini Trail. I rode that mini-bike almost every day and every day I came home I would clean it like brand new, every day. I kept the bike so clean that one day I had to take it in for service and the mechanic thought we had taken it off the showroom floor because he had never seen someone keep their mini-bike so clean after purchase. I rode my Honda Mini Trail for a few years even into my high school years.

CHAPTER 3

HIGH SCHOOL: CIGARETTES AND MARIJUANA

I was fourteen years old when I took my first puff from a cigarette at my best friend Greg's house who lived across the alley from my old house in NE DC. Greg was the first neighbor I met and he became my best friend. We played in our backyards every day until my family moved to Maryland. My parents smoked and so did Greg's mother, and by then I thought, *"How bad can it be?"* Besides, it seemed cool sharing a cigarette among the guys outside during break now. However, I had no idea the trouble it would bring me or my parents years later. As usual, one vice led to another...so from cigarettes, I went to smoking marijuana, because again, the cool guys were doing it and I wanted to try it out. And even cooler, was that my older brother, Steve, was also smoking cigarettes and weed (marijuana). Now I'm moving up in the world and it was getting cooler all the time!

During my high school years, the friends in my neighborhood, Larry, Vernel, Frank, Mitch, and Sadye, were a year or two older than I and were among the few Black families in the neighborhood. Most of the friends I hung out with drank wine and beer and smoked either cigarettes or weed or both. It just seemed like it was the thing to do. I was the *"little guy"* who they liked having around. There were always parties to go to every weekend, especially during the summer. There was one guy, Kevin, who had the only a car to take six or seven of us to all the house parties on weekends. We would always go to the store first and buy wine and someone always had the weed. I didn't like wine or beer however because it made people sick and I didn't like the taste so much… then.

HERE'S WHAT YOU NEED TO KNOW…

Even though we got high and drank beer and/or wine we were not high school drop-outs or dead beats. All of us graduated high school with good grades and went on to college or the military and have been very successful in our careers. However, this is the life we lived and the time we lived in. We were *"functional"* addicts, if considered addicts at all in those days. We were doing what everyone else did or mostly everyone else did in those days to party. The real *"addicts"* were heroin addicts that shot up with needles, etc.

I remember a time when my older brother came home from college and after he went out for the evening I looked through his suitcase for the *"big boy clothes"* to go out to a party. You know the cool guy college clothes. While looking through his suitcase I found a big bag of marijuana and helped myself to a little bit of his stash. Steve had gone to meet up with his friends and I went to Frank's house to smoke some. Boy was it was really potent! I remember playing ping pong with his brother, Mitch, who was trying to give me a hard time, in a playful way. We were all good friends. Frank, Mitch, and Sadye had the coolest parents! Their mother would walk right in the basement room where we were smoking weed and just *"push the smoke from her face"* but never said a word. We were all just blown away that she never said anything. Of course, we were all paranoid from the weed but we all kept on getting high.

So one day while my parents were away shopping, I asked my brother for some weed. He said, *"Naw, I can't do that to my brother.*

I don't want to get you started." So I pulled out my little pipe and showed him, *"I've already started smoking so you don't have to worry about that."* So my brother and his friend Skip laughed about the fact that I was getting high now and gave me a pinch of his stash. I left the house and went down the street to Frank's and told him I had some weed. So we took a walk to our friend, Larry's and decided to take a hit on the way. As we approached this one corner we had puffed out the smoke and put the pipe away when a police car pulled right in front of us at the stop sign. Our hearts were racing but the officer saw nothing. We just kept walking and proceeded on our way when our paranoia kicked into overdrive! It did not dawn on me that God was intervening in my life already, but He was. I never imagined the consequences of my life if I had gotten caught with drugs. And even when my parents discovered that my older brother smoked weed, they didn't seem to be bothered or at least say much about it. After all, my brother and his friends seemed normal. He was in school and made pretty good grades and even stood out among the university's students. To them, it was just a *"phase he was going through."* It never dawned on my parents that I was smoking marijuana also or they would have *"gone through the roof!"* as my mother used to say. It may have been okay for my brother, but not her baby! I guess there were things that older brothers could do (always) that little brothers can't or should never do… **EVER.**

CHAPTER 4

MY FIRST REAL JOB

I was fourteen years old when I got my first job as a dishwasher at a local restaurant and bar, Fred's Inn, located at Twelfth and Monroe Streets, NE, right across the street from St. Anthony's, the church I used to walk to on Sunday mornings. So my friend, Greg was the cook, at fifteen years old passing for eighteen. The owner knew he wasn't *"really"* eighteen. I was spending the night one weekend and Greg called his house while at work and asked if I wanted to work because they needed a dishwasher. I literally ran almost a mile away non-stop until getting to the backdoor entrance. The owner, Fred, took one look at me and said, *"He looks pretty young."* Greg replied, *"He's sixteen."*

"Okay, we'll give him a try." So I was shoved in front of a professional dishwasher with no experience and this became my first professional occupation. I was earning $20 a night for Friday, Saturday and Sunday evenings during the summer. The waiters were a bit older, in their twenties and no one seemed to notice my real age. They were cool though I thought because they smoked weed and drank beer. This was a lifestyle that embraced cigarettes, drugs and alcohol and it was all around me. And yet, everything seemed *"normal."* Nothing to see here. Keep moving…

Greg and I were the *"weekend team"* and basically ran the kitchen the entire weekend. Boy, it was great. We got to eat whatever we wanted, which meant *"Pizza for dinner every day!"* and a few crab cakes and steaks every now and then. When our buddies in the neighborhood found out we ran the kitchen, they could come in a group of at least four to five and expect the *"Royal Treatment."* That meant, if they ordered a cheese pizza, they expected us to hide pepperoni, onions, peppers, and the works under the cheese as if the waiters would not know. We would normally have to cut big circles from the logs of cheese for the pizza, but for our friends, we grated the cheese. It got so bad that one of the waiters noticed the *"special treatment"* given to our friends and commented, *"Too bad, all the pizzas don't look this good!"* However, the owner gave us special instructions to put four slices of cheese on all the pizzas, period. But it's amazing, even after all the extra work we put into serving our pals, they went around telling people we didn't treat them right, and we didn't *"serve them up"* as we'd say. So when we heard that, we stopped the *"special treatment"* and served them like anyone else. It's one thing to ask for more than what you paid for, but then, to be ungrateful after you've gotten it... Well, we weren't having that.

Our careers as the kitchen crew lasted about two months into our senior year in high school, when the owner decided he was paying us too much and decided that he was going to pay the both us $25 to split between the two of us! Well, rather than argue with him, because we knew that he knew that we were really underage working in a restaurant that served beer and alcohol, what could we do? Well, we did what two young teenagers do best. We ate! So every night, we would treat ourselves to a *"large pizza"* and eat one or two slices and then throw the rest away. Or we treated ourselves to a *"surf and turf"* dinner and the most expensive food in the freezer! So we made up our losses easily.

Finally, one Sunday, we decided, *"You know what... I just don't feel like going to work anymore."* So we resigned our positions as the kitchen staff by not showing up to work at Fred's Inn ever again.

SIDE NOTE: To all the young people who may read this. Let me be clear: **This is not the right way to quit a job or how to handle things when you have been wronged.** There is always a right and wrong way to do things, and this was wrong, period. Showing preference to friends, stealing, and basically robbing the owner of his goods is no way to exact revenge on someone who has done you wrong. We could have just made our petition known for a fair wage and/or quit and remained faithful to God as we represented him. I know, it is easy to make excuses for our behavior, but the fact is, there were none.

CHAPTER 4A

DISCOVERING CREATIVE WRITING

So my two favorite classes in high school were Creative Writing and the Art and Drawing. Mr. Mumford was the Creative Writing teacher at Archbishop Carroll High School in NE DC who really inspired me to really explore the depths of writing and visualize my words. Some of my stories were strange, etc., but I truly enjoyed doing the assignments every week. This was in the days of the good old *"electric typewriters"* with no *"undo"* or *"save"* features so you could start your work and come back later. It was all or nothing type of projects! I started many of them on a Friday evening and would stay up all weekend typing page after page until I had my story written and two sets of revisions! Mr. Mumford at least gave me credit for writing my own work and providing the corrected versions and the final. He would allow me to leave class and go to the Art Classroom to draw and paint since all of my assignments were complete. What a great inspiration he was and still is. Many of my artistic inspirations were due to the greatest guitarist who ever played, Jimi Hendrix, who was indeed my idol. I would smoke some weed and listen to his music and just stare at his posters all over my room and try to imagine him playing. I first heard Hendrix in the sixth grade with my friend, Tom, who lived next door to my best friend, Greg. He had the **"Monterey Pop Live Album"** and when it got to the part where Hendrix set the guitar on fire, Tom said, *"He's sacrificing his guitar!"* I was in awe of the sounds and trying to comprehend *"sacrifice his guitar"*! By the time I was in college, I collected over 150 posters and an array of albums, including an assortment of underground bootleg live albums and called my collection, *The Jimi Hendrix Memorial Museum*. So that phrase, *"Sacrificed his guitar"* stuck in my mind all the way through college and beyond!

I used to love getting high and imitating Jimi Hendrix' moves on the guitar. I would pick up a broom or anything that resembled a guitar and just have fun. Finally, I decided to purchase a cheap imitation guitar that looked like his infamous Fender Stratocaster to get the real effect. I would watch movies like Monterrey Pop, Rainbow Bridge or Woodstock and see his flamboyant gyrations with the guitar and then play the record and imitate his moves. This became a very popular past time for me. When all else failed, throw on some Hendrix and jam! Little did I know that one day my years of practicing his moves would pay off! Will share those details a little later.

CHAPTER 5

MET THE LOVE OF MY LIFE AND DIDN'T KNOW IT

In the midst of all these 70's summer days, my neighbor, Bill, who lived around the corner was another friend who had very nice parents. Bill was an only-child who had some very cool stuff; his own drum set and most of all, his own car. We did a lot of things together like; played basketball, football and baseball when the seasons permitted. One summer day in 1975, we decided to go over some nearby friends' house and see if they wanted to play basketball. I was sixteen years old and sporting a huge afro! That was the style back then. Mine was comparable to Angela Davis. (If you don't know who she is, you just don't know. Google her!) So we pulled up to our friend's house and his younger sister was outside with two friends who were very cute! We jumped out of the car like Crocket and Tubbs from the television show, Miami Vice. I looked at Bill and said, *"Who is that?!"* with emphasis! Meanwhile, little did I know that one of the girls, the older of two sisters, Minerva (now my wife), said the exact same thing to her friend! We hung out with our friends for a while talking with them and later left.

Well, the next day Bill and I went on the hunt, and mind you, this was long before the days of GPS and social media. This was just good ol' *"blood hound"* tracking. We had no address or phone number to find Minerva or her sister, but had an idea they were in the neighborhood. After driving around for about a half an hour, we pulled up to this house just a few blocks from mine. Like the gentlemen that we were, we kindly knocked on the door and to our surprise, Minerva answered the door. We stayed for a few minutes and left since her parents weren't home. You didn't do that back then. If the parents weren't home you waited until they came home, for the most part. Minerva and I became very good friends. I would visit with her for hours at a time until her father would say to us; *"Minerva. Do you know what time it is?"* That was our indication it was time for me to go home. I was two years older than she was so when I was a senior in high school she was a sophomore. However, we knew we were close and that did not matter. She was such a cutie and she was my friend. When it came time for me to go to college, we promised to stay in touch. Minerva wrote me several times while I was away at school in Baltimore and to this day, I still have all the letters she wrote me and kept them safe in a little box. Minerva knew that I smoked cigarettes, but did not know about the drugs I did. I kept that secret from her. I was afraid that she would have nothing to do with me if she found out that I got high. So I saved my *"bad boy"* behavior for other friends. We ended up dating other people but always remained good friends. Then I disappeared into college days seeing her occasionally during holidays.

CHAPTER 6

COLLEGE DAYS

By the time I got into college smoking cigarettes and weed was just part of my life, as it was with many of my friends. Just about everyone in college got high, including the instructors. Occasionally you would find someone who didn't smoke weed, but that wasn't the norm. One weekend there was a festival at Morgan State College, where my brother was attending, and I spent the whole time there with some friends. While hanging out in the girl's dorm, a girl-friend opened up a capsule and snorted this white powder and asked me if I wanted to try it. So I asked her, *"That isn't cocaine is it?"* She said, *"No, it's speed."* So I figured, as long as it wasn't something hard, like cocaine, then what the heck. So I took a sniff in each nostril and it had a sort of *"kick"* to it. The next thing I know I felt *"lifted up"* with energy. Well the three friends and I, stayed up all weekend long, with no sleep partying at the festival with nothing to eat all weekend long. Finally, that Sunday, I said we could get something to eat at my brother's place. So the three of us hitch-hiked to his apartment, about three miles away, and basically waited to get something to eat. I remember walking in the kitchen and all of a sudden I saw nothing but *"white"* and fell up against the stove and almost blacked out. This had never happened to me before and I was a bit scared over the experience. Fortunately, no one saw me and my cover wasn't blown and I said nothing about what happened.

I spent two years studying art at The Maryland Institute College of Art meeting fellow students, partying and learning from some real masters at drawing and painting. One day a guy who always seemed a little weird talked about doing LSD. He made it sound so much fun and whimsical and there was nothing to it because he did it all the time. He mentioned one time he took it and went to an animated movie and when he came outside the theater everything looked like a cartoon! It was the craziest experience and he said I would love it! He told me he was about to put in an order for some *"Red Dragon"* from California and wanted to know if I wanted any. I was hesitant for a few days. But I finally told him to get me two of them. So my girlfriend, Renee, back home in Silver Spring, MD, and I planned to take it over the upcoming weekend to experiment with it. A few days later the guy gave me two small pieces of small paper with the *"red stains"* on them and warned me saying, *"You're going to be up all day and night. Don't plan on doing much but tripping!"*

So my girlfriend arrived that Friday evening at the Greyhound bus station. We had dinner and a good night sleep since we were going to be up all night according to my school mate. The next day, we started by taking only half of the LSD…about an hour or two later we took the other halves because we didn't feel anything. But about an hour after that the strange sensations of the Red Dragon started to kick in…and then, it was on! We stayed on that hallucinogenic ride all-day, way into the night! The colors were so intense, melting frames and things that just came out of nowhere. It was a visual experience like I had never had before! There were faces in everything that were just regular objects and our minds were opened up to them. We looked at drawings I did, album covers, cracks in the wall, clouds and more! We had never seen such things and it was everywhere! It rained that day so we decided to stay inside because we didn't know if the rain would freak us out. It was indeed a ride…not one that I would recommend though. LSD has some very long-lasting effects and it is a very dangerous drug, though many may beg to differ. Any *"mind-altering"* drug is harmful to the mind, body and spirit that opens what is called, *"The Third Eye."* I have found too, that *"experimenting with drugs"* is not an experiment that you want to take chances. As a volunteer chaplain that worked in a Mental Health Unit at a local hospital, I have seen many people who landed there after *"experimenting with heroin"* for the very first time and ended up addicted to the drug for years. **ANY DRUG CAN BE DANGEROUS, especially if abused.** Please do not attempt to use drugs without a prescription and/or without a doctor's instruction and supervision.

That summer, after my second school semester at the Maryland Institute of Art in Baltimore, I moved back home and transferred to The Corcoran School of Art, in Washington, DC. I completed two and a half years there where I received my Bachelor's Degree in Graphic Design in 1981.

CHAPTER 7

SUMMER JOB:
THE DEPARTMENT OF THE INTERIOR

In the summer of 1980, after I came home from Baltimore my mother called me in her room and said, *"You're not going to sit around and do nothing all summer. You're going to have to get a job."* So Mom called one of her very dear friends, Harry T, who worked at the Department of the Interior and just said, *"Harry, my youngest son, Greg, needs a job. Can you help him out?"* Harry replied, *"Send him down to me Phyllis. I'll take care of him."* So the very next day, I found myself taking the Metro downtown to the Department of the Interior where I met Mr. Harry T. What a delightful guy! He always had a smile and seemed to know everyone in the building and in town! And when I say *"Everyone I mean EVERYONE!"* and even if he didn't know you, he spoke to you as if he did!

Harry took me in to meet the office manager and informed him that I would be working with him for the summer. We were a small department of about eight or nine people, but it was great because now, I had a job! So I went to the HR Department to fill out the infamous 171 Form, where you basically give every bit of information about yourself except your blood type, and maybe that too! So I worked this job every summer with Harry T and gang. However, you would not believe back in the early 1980s just how many people were getting high *"inside and outside"* of the

Department of the Interior! Oh my goodness! People were just bold…self-included. We'd smoke weed in the bathrooms or go up on the maintenance floors and sit in huge crates and get high. It didn't matter. And the folks who were the outdoor *"regulars"* they would go over to the park across the street regularly during the day and smoke and drink beer and alcohol. They could have filled a tractor trailer with the number of people getting high every day. And the thing is… EVERYONE knew about it. No one said a word. It was just a thing.

One day, while walking the hall at DOTI, a guy I knew asked me if I was in school for graphic design. When I told him *"Yes,"* he informed me that I could get on a special program they had for students and do an internship. The great thing about this program is, not only would I get credit for it in school and not only would I get paid, but they would give me a full-time job right after graduation with a *"pay raise"*! OUTSTANDING! So I signed up for it.

CHAPTER 8

INTERNSHIP:
THE DEPARTMENT OF THE INTERIOR

This is where my future as a graphic designer really took off! So I was assigned to work in another office a few blocks away from the Main Building. There I met the art director, Peter DuFóre. Pete was indeed a *"true artist"* in every sense of the word. He was a flamboyant-dressing native New Yorker from Hell's Kitchen (The Real Hell's Kitchen, NY) with his bright blue Hawaiian shirts, blue turquois beads and bangles he wore every day. He was a musician and trumpet player who fancied the New York night club scenes with such virtuosos as: Miles Davis Dizzy Gillespie and others. Pete was also a Vietnam veteran that he took very seriously. I met him when I was twenty years old and a junior at the Corcoran School of Art in NW DC, right across from the White House. Pete used to tell me how much I reminded him of himself when he was my age. He used to call me *"A young whipper snapper!"* all the time! I learned some of the most valuable lessons from my dear friend and mentor Pete. I learned how to use a PosOne Photostat camera, Compu-Graphic Typesetting Machine and I watched him do paste-up work like a surgeon. He was so precise I used to call him *"The Doctor!"* to which he graciously accepted…with honors!

Pete showed me the ropes on how to do professional layout and paste-up work for the government and he was always so direct but very cool. He was as they say, *"Chill."* One thing that he used to tell me a lot and I never forgot was: *"You got some dues to pay brother."*

"You don't understand what I'm talking about yet. But one day you will." I didn't know what he was talking about then. But a few years later I found out. And boy, did I pay some dues, but I'll tell you about that later. It was a car accident that happened in 1983… just FYI.

One Saturday afternoon, I was playing my imitation Fender Strat guitar and wrote this song that I liked so much that I called Pete so I could play it for him to get his opinion. I had never called his house before and when he answered I could tell he was a bit hesitant, *"Uhhh yeah…what's up?"*

"Hey, Pete, I just wanted to play this song for you and see what you think?"

"You called because you wanted to play a song for me? REALLY? Man, no one's ever done that for me! Everyone who calls usually calls because they want something. Man, what a friend. You can call me anytime!" So I understood Pete to be a very private guy at home.

Pete stayed to himself and his family and I guess for good reason, especially if people only called because they wanted something. He was just a very cool guy who I wanted to get to know better and enjoy our friendship. You could tell by talking with him that he knew a lot about a lot. He had tons on his mind and you just had to get it out of him. I have a lot of respect and love for this guy.

I remember the first time I visited Pete and his wonderful family down in Dale City, VA. I met his wife, Maxine, and two daughters, Danielle and Shaanna, who were extremely accepting of this young guy that worked with their dad. When I walked in the front door, there were paintings of all sizes all over the house. I mean *"all over the house! Everywhere!"* I thought they were just huge collectors of art and I casually said to Pete, *"Nice collection you have. Whose work is it?"* Pete looked dismayed and said, *"What do you mean whose? They're mine!"* I was floored! These paintings belonged in a museum! I mean, they were absolutely incredible! I never knew Peter Michael DuFóre was such a talented artist and painter! His paintings were so expressive and detailed and colorful! WOWWW!

Pete followed my career and always called me his *"protégé."* He was very proud that he had a huge influence over my life and my career. He was the first to teach me things about Graphic Design outside the classroom. And yes, we enjoyed an occasional joint at home and a rum and coke at lunch every now and then. However, the one thing that you must know about Peter Michael DuFóre and Gregory Austin Glaude is that we still hold the title record for devouring a large pepperoni pizza. Seriously! One day Pete went to our favorite bar and restaurant down the street from work and we ate this large pepperoni pizza so fast that the waitress thought we had not gotten our food! THIRTY SECONDS FLAT! Oh I'm certain there are a lot of takers today, but Pete and I loved the idea that, to this day, no one has ever beaten our record! We have claimed it and that's the way it is. Pete would brag to his family, friends and associates that he trained me during my college years which helped me land a job doing news graphics for WDVM TV 9, a local news station in Washington, DC, which he did. Pete will always be remembered dearly in my heart as a *"true artist, designer, and painter"* who left an indelible impression on me forever. Sadly, my dear friend Peter Michael DuFóre died of cancer on June 29, 2010. Everyone wore their favorite colors to honor him as we laid him to rest.

CHAPTER 9

DC101 AIR GUITAR CONTEST

In 1980, a local radio station, DC101 announced that they were having their first-ever *"Air Guitar Contest"* and first prize was a real Fender Stratocaster guitar. Every day while at school at the Corcoran School of Art, we would hear the commercials and if you were the ninth caller, you got a chance to do your air guitar to win first prize. I kept telling my friends at school.

"I know I can win this contest! I've been practicing Jimi Hendrix for years! If I could only get through the phone lines…"

It was Friday, the day before the contest and I still had not gotten through on the phone lines when they announced, *"If you can't get through on the phones, go to Peaches Records & Tape and fill out an entry form!"* So I was sitting by the radio with two other friends, Ray and Linda, and told them, *"Man! If I could get there I know I can win this contest! I know it!"* So my friend Linda said, *"Well I know where Peaches Records & Tape is. Do you want me to take you there?"*

"ABSOLUTELY!"

So we got to PR&T and we filled out a few entry forms to make sure I would get called. While we were putting the few in the box, this girl comes up and stuffs like two hundred entry forms in the box! So I asked her, *"Are all those forms for one person?"*

She replied, *"You damned right they are! I'm gonna win that guitar!"* and pointed right above our heads where the first prize guitar was hanging. Needless to say, Linda and I grabbed handfuls of forms and just wrote my name on them. That evening, I went to my dear ol' friend Mitch and told him my dilemma. I was going to be in the DC101 Air Guitar Contest tomorrow and I needed some weed to get high before the contest. He was very enthusiastic because he knew I was determined not to lose! I was representing my idol, Jimi Hendrix, so I had to be correct. That night, I parked mom's car in the driveway as usual but unusually, left a suede leather bag with several pipes I used for weed in the car. I slept in the den that night for some reason and when I woke up, the bag was on my bed…and Mom was not happy.

That morning, Linda stopped by to pick me up for the contest. I had already drank a Schlitz Malt Liquor Bull and started smoking weed to get myself prepared for the most important contest of all time. I could tell as we were leaving that mother was not pleased with me due to her *"discovery"* I left in the car and I knew that we would have words about it later. Dad seemed okay. He didn't pay much attention to it.

So when we got to Peaches Records & Tape, there were seemingly hundreds of people there including the radio announcer, Dave Brown, from DC101. When they started to draw the names from the box, they pulled my name eight times and laughed and said, *"This guy really wants to win!"* So there were seven contestants who went up before me and none of them knew any of the songs on this new album they were promoting. However, because Linda bought me the album the night before, I knew the *"sweet spot"* on the album. So when they called me up they started the song in the wrong spot and I was like *"Hold it! Hold it! You've got to start the song in the middle of the record."* You only had forty-five seconds so I had to make them count! When the song started, I gave a very flamboyant performance, just like Jimi Hendrix would have done and to finish, I jumped up in the air and landed on one knee and pointed at the guitar…and **THE CROWD WENT WILD!**

There were a total of thirty-five contestants with five finalists. Everyone used the same song I chose so that put me in the mix right there. So there were two girls and three guys for the finalists, including me. Everyone started doing their "typical invisible guitar tuning" while I just stood behind them with my eyes closed. I don't know if I was praying to the *"guitar gods, Hendrix or what,"* but I stood there silent until BAMM! The music blasts on and I ran in front of everyone to steal the show! However, when I jumped up front, there was a group of people up front and one guy was recording and they pointed to me saying I was too close and to *"Move back! Move back!"* So as I stepped back I tripped over someone's foot I went in slowwwwwwwwwwwwww moooooooootion and fell flat on my back! But I saved the day and kept rolling over and landed on my knees in classic Jimi Hendrix form! The audience was screaming and yelling and all I could see was **VICTORY!** When the song was over, people were congratulating me already and I knew it. I knew I had won that Fender Strat. Game over!

I came home from the contest with Linda and Dad asked me, *"Did you win?"* and I told him *"Of course! Never any doubt!"* And Dad was like *"Gimme five!"* However, Mom was not in the congratulatory mood and her fire was fueled even more for me winning. She felt this was why I was doing drugs and did not want to support this madness.

My friend Mitch, who gave me the joints the night before, said he had the radio station on DC101 all morning at the liquor store he worked at. When they announced me as the winner, *"Gregory Glaude of Silver Spring is the winner of the Air Guitar Contest!"* he said he went jumping up and down the aisles and couldn't believe it. But I told everyone, *"I knew I could win."* Here's the thing about our God. The Lord Jesus Christ knew one day I would call on His name, not for a contest for a guitar, but for something far more serious, my life. He knew that because of all my smoking, drinking and doing drugs that this lifestyle would take its toll on me, I would have "dues to pay" as Pete would say. So I had a lot of bragging rights for a while. Everyone heard about the DC101 Air Guitar Contest! So I proudly took the guitar from one friend to another to show them that beautiful wood grained guitar. Soon, Mom calmed down about the bag of paraphernalia and we were back on track.

CHAPTER 10

HOMEWORK VS. THE STRAT

I had another year and a half of college left and I started playing the Strat every single day for hours at a time. I was never that good, but that didn't matter. I was playing the Strat that I won. I remember coming home about midnight one evening with plenty of homework still left to do. However, the buzz I had from the weed I smoked earlier was still good to go and I wanted to just play the Strat for a half an hour...just a half. I mean I was desperate! And then it hit me.

"You have a problem. You have work to do, work for school and now you have to make a decision." So I stopped then and said to myself, *"If you're going to play the guitar, then play the guitar and be the BEST guitar player you can be. However, you're going to stop going to school for art. Whichever one you pick though, that's it! That's going to be your career."* So I did not play the guitar that night and I sat down and finished my graphic design homework. What lesson did I learn from that? Sometimes you have to make the right decision to do the right thing, even when your heart tells you to do something else. I knew I had to honor my parents who were paying my tuition for my education and the guitar was something that I enjoyed doing.

CHAPTER 11

THE BAND FOR A WEEK

So right before graduation, I met a guy, Andy, standing in line to buy Van Halen tickets. This guy starts singing "Sweet Leaf" by Black Sabbath and I joined in with him. It turned out that he was a drummer and we hooked up to jam a little bit. He knew a bass player and the three of us were pretty good at making some cool noise. We knew about three or four Black Sabbath and Jimi Hendrix songs. Did I mention too that Andy sold weed? So one day after about our third time playing together, this really nice-looking girl, Tammy, came in to buy some weed. While she was there Andy takes a phone call about a party a friend is having. He tells them, *"Hey, dude! I've got a band now and we're pretty good! We'll play at your party!"* I was thinking, no way. So Tammy asked me if I was going to play at the party and I told her, *"I'll do it if you're going to be there…but if you don't come, I'm not playing."*

So the next day, we loaded all the drums and guitar equipment in my huge Buick Supreme and went to the party. I set up in just a few minutes and then Tammy showed up. She said, *"Let's go for a ride. We'll be right back."* They guys were like, *"Man you aren't coming back! Don't leave…"* So of course, I did the right thing… Tammy and I were driving down the road smoking some weed and just laughing having a good time. The next thing I know we're sitting in front of her house. When we got back to the party the guys were ready to play so we hit our favorite song *"Sweet Leaf."* During the song I took liberty to do an extra-long guitar solo right in front of Tammy. She thanked me by putting her arms around my neck and gave me a big long kiss while I was still playing! The guys were getting jealous but it was my moment. Finally a guy, I don't know who pulled me away from the kiss and I was pretty upset but kept playing. And that's it for my band for a week. We never played again. Tammy and I broke up after a few months of partying and drinking and doing drugs. She had a very *"wild streak"* about her that I just could not keep up with. She was and probably still is a sweet girl. She loved my dad and would call him by his name, *"Criss,"* but he never knew that.

In the summer 1981, I graduated from the Corcoran School of Art and Ronald Reagan became president of the United States and part of his legacy was to eliminate many of the programs that were instituted at the time, including my job that would have been with Peter DuFóre. I would have been a full-time employee but now jobless. So I started looking for work and naturally figured it would be no time before landing a job as a *"high-paying"* graphic designer. After all, that was the plan…until reality set in. People were not hiring! So after about two months of sending out resumes I called my former girlfriend, Tammy, whose father owned a local trash company and asked her if she could get me a job. She replied, *"I'll make Daddy hire you!"* So I went down to the office and Mr. Dawes was waiting for me. He told me, *"You know Greg, I really don't need any help right now, but I know you're looking for work so I'll let you work with me until you find a job. You can start tomorrow."* So I started work on a Wednesday morning… Up at 4:00 AM, out the house by five and on the truck by 5:30 AM. I first went out with Steve, the middle brother of five. All the Dawes brothers and cousins worked the family business. Steve seemed to be one of the most *"reasonable"* and he and I got along well. We rode around for about a half an hour and then he said, *"Okay… Time to get to work."* He stayed in the truck while he pointed me to the back. I started picking up trash cans and running after the truck and I realized, this was going to be a workout for sure! Block after block, can after can, smell after nasty smell, I was hauling trash up to the truck all morning long. We got to one neighborhood and this guy came out and I was just hot and thirsty. He handed me a cold beer in a can. I took the can opened it and in one swallow downed that entire beer in about three seconds and tossed the can in the back of the truck. It was about 2:00 PM in the afternoon when we got back to the office. I was so tired and hot and I knew I had put in a hard day's work only to find out as Steve laughed at me and said, *"This was the lightest day of the week! Wait until you burlap!"* Well, I didn't know what *"burlap"* was other than a rough material or whatever. But whatever it was, it was coming on Tuesday. I went home and my tennis shoes were dirty and smelled and so did my clothes. I knew I had to prepare for battle. So I went down to the surplus store and bought some army boots, thinking these will last a while and at least tough enough to stand up to the wear and tear of the truck.

Day after day, I would come home dirty and smelly and the boots I just bought looked like they had been through combat in only a few days. Finally, Tuesday morning came and it was time to find out about *"burlappin'."* As the saying goes, *"If you don't know. You don't know."* I certainly did not know... But I was about to find out. So Gregory, the youngest brother had me ride with him. There was always a *"competition"* between the brothers about who was the strongest or the toughest or the smartest or whatever. Gregory wanted to prove to me his strength while he showed me what burlappin' was. So we went into the basement of this apartment building and Gregory unraveled this huge piece of burlap and threw it on the floor. Then he took three or four trashcans and dumped the trash in the middle of the burlap and made a huge pile. Then he grabbed one corner, then another, then another and then the last corner. He pulled them together and then rolled it over and threw this huge lump of burlap trash over his shoulder and just walked up the steps! He was indeed my hero! When we got upstairs to the truck, he grabbed one corner and threw the rest and it opened up like a fireworks of trash flying into the back of the truck. I was amazed! He threw me a big piece of burlap and said, *"Get that building over there. I'll get the other one."* I was thinking, *"And you want me to do this by myself?"* This truly was trial by trash! I went in the basement of that building. I threw the burlap down okay. I even threw the trash on top okay. However, when it came to lifting that huge mass of stink and mess over my shoulder…we now had a problem. About twenty minutes went by and Gregory came looking for me and to his dismay, I was still trying to lift this burlap sack of trash and mess. Gregory got disgusted and grabbed the bag from me and carried it out to the truck. *"You gonna have to learn burlappin' if you want to work here"* is all he said. So this was my routine. Up by 4:00 a.m., out the house by 4:30 a.m., then at work by 5:00 a.m. and by 6:00 a.m. I was hauling trash six days a week for two weeks. I would get home around 3:00 or 4:00 p.m. and smelled like trash—I mean, smelly stinky trash. I would take a shower and change and try to go hang out with the fellas in the old neighborhood at the playground. Every neighborhood has the *"playground"* hangout. This is where my buddies were after work during the summer. We'd hang out and drink a few beers, etc. By 7:00 p.m., I was so tired I had to just go home and get in the bed so I could rest for the next day of work. Hard work. Like the Bible says, *"By the sweat of your brow"* kind of work.

So after three hard weeks of trash hauling, stinks and smells, I went in the office and got my paycheck on Saturday. I told Mr. Dawes that I had found a job and they wanted me to start on Monday. I thanked him for his time and generosity and wished him well. That Monday, I got up early and grabbed, that's right, you guessed it… The Yellow Pages. The real Yellow Pages and started calling every phone number under *"graphic design."* For three days I called from morning until evening, about thirty calls a day. Finally, at the end of Wednesday, a woman asked me if I could come in for an interview the next day, and I did, and got my first graphic design job since school. Now here is where I tell you that *"internships pay off!"* So after about a month working at this little paste-up house for government work, I noticed that they had sitting in the corner, a POS ONE Photostat camera, just like the one

I learned on with my ol' buddy Pete from The Department of the Interior, and no one was using it. It had a little rust on the inside but otherwise looked good. I informed the owner that I thought I could fix the stat camera and get it working, and so I did.

Meanwhile, a dear friend, Paula, from my neighborhood called me one night and said, *"Hey, Greg, I'm working at Channel 9 News and they have an opening in their graphics department. Are you interested?"*

"Absolutely I am!" So I called the guy and went in for an interview on a Monday. However, by Wednesday I had not heard back from the guy so I called him up and said, *"Hey listen, I really want this job. I don't know what I can do to prove it, but let me know because I want to work there."* He replied, *"Well you just did. Out of all the others I interviewed, you were the only one who called back. You're hired."*

CHAPTER 12

MY THIRD JOB: WDVM TV

You become very popular when your friends see your name on television. That's all I'm going to say. The mystique behind television is amazing. It's like learning all the magician's tricks and now you have the secrets! So after about a year working at the station, I heard my coworker ask a woman in another department for sales about some *"tickets for the Capital Centre"* which was a big deal back then. So I asked her about the tickets and she said, *"Yes, we have Sky Suite at Capital Centre and you can get tickets for any event. Just ask."* And so I did ask and got a ticket to a Bullets Basketball game. Boy I thought I was a big shot! Here I was showing up to this event with other big wigs and I'm there watching this game in the Sky Suite. Well as the saying goes which I just made up, *"You even get used to a Rolls Royce if you drive it long enough."*

After about a couple of months of different events and such, I found out something very important. Of all the events that they have at the Capital Centre, NO ONE GOES TO ROCK CONCERTS! Soon, the lady upstairs became my buddy with the tickets and she would call me and ask, *"Hey, Greg, I have ten tickets for the Friday night show and eleven for the Saturday night show...do you want them all?"*

"I sure do!" I took the Friday tickets down to Georgetown and sold them right in front of, for those who remember, The Crazy

Horse, bar and grille. There was one guy however that I'm glad I wasn't scamming. This was the biggest white guy I've ever seen. He looked at the ticket and said, *"It looks real enough. But if it isn't, the world is a small place."* And was like, *"Dude, if that was a fake ticket I'd take it back right now! Go have a good time!"* I never saw him again, but I know he went there and had a blast!

Let me tell you, I was pretty good at keeping my drug addictions to myself. If you knew about me getting high it's because I let you know I got high. Otherwise, I could keep my *"ups and downs"* pretty well hidden. However, I didn't realize how many people got high at Channel 9 television station until I went to a party after work one evening. One of the news reporters was retiring and everyone there seemed to be looking for either weed or coke (cocaine) or both. And what was more interesting is the number of people who were hooking up. So in the middle of all this, I was getting tickets to every rock concert that came to Capital Centre and every popular group from Black Sabbath, Heart, Judas Priest, you name them, I was getting free sky suite tickets. Every other week, my buddy, Greg, would call the station. *"Hey, man! You going to the show this weekend? You got me right? Yeah, Tom's going too?"* It was no problem for me to get a handful of tickets for the shows.

I remember the first time we went there. I don't remember who we were seeing. But I do remember the *"liquor store"* we had in the trunk of the car! I remember the coke I snorted and weed I smoked on the way. I remember being in the parking lot drinking and the cops were pretty cool because as long as we weren't acting *"real stupid"* they'd leave us alone. There were special elevators that took us upstairs to the sky suites. Once we got to our floor, the waiters checked our tickets and showed us our room. When the door opened, we just lost it. This was luxury partying at its best and we were the only ones in the suite. What made it worse, you could order drinks up there. So of course we had to imbibe. Tom, as only Tom would do, asked to buy a *"bottle of vodka."* The waiter was nice and said, *"Sir, we can only sell the alcohol by the shot."* And of course, Tom's reply was, *"Well, how many shots are in the bottle? I'll pay that…"* So after about ten minutes of going back and forth, he agreed to buy three or four shots and waited to see if he wanted any more. We finished the evening with a neighbor in another sky suite who offered us **FREE BEER,** from their keg and unfortunately, we had no cups. So we, as creative thinking goes, improvised by emptying a bucket of popcorn to replace it with ice cold beer. All I can say is *"ONLY BY THE GRACE OF GOD"* did we make it home safely. I was not kidding when I said, you are reading the words of someone who should be dead and that the number of times the Lord Jesus Christ spared my life are more than I could know. Truly, what I am about to tell you is one of those times.

So fast forward a little. After high school, Frank had joined the Navy, his parents and sister, Sadye, had moved away to Memphis, Tennessee, and their brother, Mitch, stayed and got an apartment nearby and worked for a liquor store. I would drive down to Columbia Road in Adams Morgan to his store right around closing and we would sit in the back, have a beer or two, smoke a joint and then head home.

After a few years, Frank had finished his time in the Navy and moved back home. One rainy night, we jumped in his scruffy blue Datsun B210 decided to go to the University of Maryland because, as usual, we heard there was a party there. So we decided to investigate. After circling the campus a while we heard from some young ladies there was a big party down in DC on 16th Street, N.W. So with nothing else to do we smoked a joint on the way and went flying down the road in the little *"café racer."* As we were approaching 16th Street, N.W., the light turned yellow and Frank stepped on the pedal to make the light and the left turn. We made the light, but not the left turn and on the wet pavement, the Datsun kept going straight, right over the curb! The car slid over the curb and between two or three trees that we could have smashed into. After sliding for several yards we came to a stop. Frank looked at me and

I looked at him and we knew we had dodged a huge bullet. Frank took a breath and said, *"You okay?"*

"Yeah you?" We sat there a second and then we both just jumped out of the car like it just happened...it was a delayed reaction. When we examined the car there was no damage but we had two flat tires and the very long skid marks in the grass which was evidence that God indeed intervened and spared our lives. But what did we know? We just thought we were *"damn lucky."* I mean how could we slide probably over one hundred feet on wet pavement, go over a curb, continue sliding and miss three trees and walk away without a scratch? I now know that this was one of those times of the Lord Jesus' interventions. He had plans for me and I didn't know it yet.

"For I know the thoughts that I think toward you, says the Lord, thoughts of peace and not of evil, to give you a future and a hope." *(Jeremiah 29:11)*

So we walked to the nearest phone booth leaving the Datsun B210 lawn sculpture in place as a memento of our evening. We called Mitch to see if he would pick us up and relieve us from our dilemma. However, as typical with him, he wanted to make the point that we were foolish for driving too fast in the rain and our punishment was to walk home. So about an hour or so later we got back to Mitch's apartment and drank a beer and smoked a joint or two in protest of the evening's troubles.

A few years later Frank met the love of his life, Charlotte "Faye." One evening while walking up the stairs to Mitch's apartment, Frank announced that he and Faye were getting married. Well, a few months later Sadye, Frank and Mitch's sister, came in town for the wedding and she never looked better. During the wedding reception we were all talking about Sadye moving back to Maryland and how much fun we were having! So after about a few months, Sadye did indeed move back and was living with Mitch.

Sadye had a boyfriend here in Maryland but I didn't care about that as I was dating someone else too. However, Sadye and I were getting closer to one another and it just felt right. That New Year's Eve of 1982 going into 1983, Mitch had a party at his apartment and everyone was there. Right at midnight she looked at me and gave me a little kiss and then we danced. I remember the dance and how close we were and I knew it then.

As the next few weeks went by, Sadye would call me at the station on Friday nights, to meet her at the latest club. Since I got off work at 11:30 PM, it was no problem. I would catch up with her after work, have some drinks and dance and just have a good ol' time.

On Wednesday, March 9, 1983, Mitch called me around 9:00 AM to see if I would take him to pick his car up from a service place in SE DC. I was happy to help my friend. In appreciation for my time, he took me to breakfast. While enjoying our food I disclosed a secret to him. *"Man. I've got something to tell you."*

"What's that?"

"I'm in love."

"Okay… Who's the lucky lady?"

"It's Sadye."

"Whaaaatt!? I knew it! I knew it!"

"She's been bouncing around the apartment and I couldn't tell what was going on with her! Now I know!"

"Well, Mitch. I want to ask her to marry me."

"Man. Greg! I would be honored to have you as my brother! I don't think you're going to have a problem! She's been telling these guys

that she's been seeing, 'They better get used to you being around!' So I know she's going to say yes." It meant so much to me to have his blessing and to hear that she would accept. This was such good news!

CHAPTER 13

FRIDAY, MARCH 11, 1983

Friday evening came and Sadye asked if we could go to a new nightclub that she hadn't been to before, *"The Classics"* off of the Beltway 495 near Andrew's AFB. She asked another friend, Grace, if she wanted to go with us around 9:30 PM. We waited for Grace for an hour or more and she finally arrived around 11pm. The Classics was about a forty-five minute drive away. When we arrived at the club we pulled into a very narrow parking lot, to which we were informed that it was full. I said to the girls, *"Boy this place is packed! We're never going to get in. Maybe we should come back tomorrow a little earlier."* But the girls pleaded with me, *"C'mon! Please! We're here now! Let's just go in and see what it's like since we're here."* So against my better judgment, I said, *"Okay. We'll go in for a bit."* This place was so popular there were no spaces available in the lot and cars parked all the way down this dark road for at least a quarter mile. We walked all the way back up this dark road to the lights on the other side of the road way to the club's entrance. Right as we crossed the street to go in the club, I had each girl on my left and right side and said, *"Tonight, you all are going to be my bodyguards."* I didn't realize how true these words would come to be. So we went in and ordered a couple of drinks and then a slow song came on and I asked Sadye to dance and I felt so close to her. When the song was over, I looked in her eyes and said, *"Sadye... I..."* She looked at me as if she knew what I was going to say, but maybe not ready to hear me say it and said, *"I'll be right back."* So we partied a while longer.

So after two hours of drinks and dancing, the club was closing and we started down the parking lot and back to the car, which was about a quarter of a mile down the road across the four-lane roadway. It was pretty far away. When we were stepping into the roadway there were two lanes for each direction. I looked down the road to the left and all I saw was the dark black emptiness of the night. There were no lights to illuminate the road. I turned to look to the right while we started to cross the road only seeing tiny dim headlights far away. So I said to the girls, *"Let's hurry up and cross the street."* So I grabbed one in each arm and we ran, kind of laughing. *"Let's hurry!"*

So as we stepped into the last lane I looked up to the right and was smothered by the bright headlights right on top of us! I threw my arms up to push the girls back. BAAAAMMM! The three of us were hit and were scattered across the road like little rag dolls. The impact threw me in the air then sent me tumbling over in the middle of the road, rolling over and over and over and over and over and over and over and over and over. I rolled so many times only seeing the full moon against the black sky and the darkness of the road that I thought to myself, *"When am I going to stop!?"* I finally came to a stop in the middle of Allentown Road. I heard the screeching of tires coming to an abrupt stop and the sound of gravel being shuffled on the side. There was a pause of silence. Then I heard the sound of tires racing off into the night echoed against this backdrop of horror. The guy who hit us left us for dead in the road! It was a hit-and-run accident. *"Someone go after him! He's getting away!"* More screams bellowed out *"Ohhhh nooo! Oh my God! Someone help them!"* As I laid there still in the middle of the street I was consumed by the fear that I could be run over a second time. If the guy couldn't see us standing up, how will anyone see me flat on my back? Then the only thing I could think was, *"This is BAD. This is REALLY BAD…"* I couldn't determine yet if the girls were hit by the car. Did I push them out of the way in time? Then the thought of them being hit started to give me a horrible feeling. Then the pain started to set in. It rose up my leg like heat and I realized I may be severely injured. My legs could have been broken and all I thought then was *"Don't try to move. You don't want to move and make it worse."* I realized that the girls must have been hit too because I didn't hear them. I know they would have come to me if they weren't hit. I looked immediately around me and didn't see them. Then it dawned on me, *"They're not near you. Look down the road."* As I tried to look further, I lifted my head struggling not to move my body too much, to my dismay, I found the faint silhouette of a body folded over was lying face down in the middle of the road and I couldn't tell who it was. My heart started to race even more. She was not moving. Was she dead? I couldn't tell.

Finally, a man came up to me and asked me if I was okay. I told him I was and asked, *"How are the girls?"* He wouldn't respond but told me to hold on and hang in there. This terrified me even more because I couldn't find the other girl. Neither of them were saying anything or crying out. From the cold of the early morning and the fear of losing both girls, I trembled and shook and shock was setting in. The impact of the car knocked off one of my shoes and my foot was cold. I still had not found my other friend and I knew she had to have been hit because I didn't hear her voice. So I looked down the road again. I looked to my left side and I looked to my right and nothing. Finally, I saw a group of people gathered near a car. Why were they there I thought. Is that where my friend was, near the car? As I tried to see any evidence of life, I finally saw a foot that was protruding from underneath the car…that had to be my friend. She was thrown under a parked car. My heart just sank into the ground and I just wanted to black out. I didn't want to see anymore! *"How could this happen?"*

"WHYYYYY?" Then it dawned on me. *"You're going to have to tough it out. You're the only one who's alive and conscious and can give someone your family's and Mitch's contact info. You're going to have to hang in there and stay awake."* The time passed so slowly as I was shivering and freezing laying on that cold ground…

By now, the Prince George's County Police arrived. This young Black officer came to me and had the look of authority in his eyes and asked *"How are you doing son?"*

"I'm okay." The officer told me, *"You're pretty brave son. Hang in there."* Then I told the officer that he had to contact my parents and my friend, Mitch. I gave him the phone numbers thinking, *"Ohhh no. What are they going to think? How horrible is it to get that phone call at 3:00 AM in the morning that your loved ones have been in an accident?"* Worse yet, is I still didn't know if the girls were alive or dead. No one would tell me. Soon after, an ambulance arrived and the paramedics started to load me onto a gurney and then placed me in the back of the ambulance. I told them I wanted to wait to see how my friends were doing. But they said, *"You have the least amount of injuries. We have to take you first."* So I left the scene of the accident that would change my life forever, looking out the back window as the scene faded away.

When we arrived at Southern Maryland Hospital the attendants took me out of the ambulance and reported that I had been hit by a car. I was placed in a room and waited for a bit until the technician came and took me to X-ray my legs and back. The pain was still like heat running up and down my legs so it was difficult for me to maneuver. When he was done he returned me to my room. To all of our amazement, I didn't have one broken bone, given the fact that I had just been hit by a car travelling 65mph. There was no way I could get hit by a car at full impact, and not break a bone. I was just relieved somehow that I wasn't injured further. Sometime later, both my parents showed up at the hospital around 4 AM and gave me the look of relief to know that I was sitting up in the bed in the emergency room. I knew they must have been going through hell all the way to the hospital. Seeing me alive and well, for the most part and knowing my condition wasn't worse eased their minds. We waited about another hour or so before the doctor showed up and released me to go home.

It was 7:00 AM Saturday morning the nurse wheeled out to my mom's car and the attendants lifted me in the car, placed me on the back seat and we drove off. The sun was up and I was still trying to make sense of all the horrible events that had taken place only a few hours before. We got on the Beltway 495 and started to head down the road and soon we passed The Classics nightclub. I looked over the roadway and I could still see my car in the same place where I had parked it hours before. My heart sunk again thinking about the girls and not knowing their condition or whereabouts. When we got home, Mom and Dad lifted me up and carried me in the house all the way back to my bedroom in the back of the house and laid me in my bed. I said to my mother, *"Mom, you have to go check on the girls. I don't know if they are alive or dead. No one would tell me anything at the accident and I am afraid. Please go check on them."*

It was around 9:00 AM when Mom left the house. She didn't return until 5:30 PM that evening and she said, *"Greg. I have news about the girls... They're both alive, but they are banged up really bad."* Well, that was relief to my ears! They were both alive! That's all I needed to hear. That was the HOPE I was looking for. Banged up just means you're going to have to take some time to heal. Better than dead. However, I didn't know the extent of *"Banged up"* that mom meant. Later, Saturday evening Greg and Tom came by after hearing the news of the accident. They both showed up with two grocery bags of beer and liquor so we could get drunk and forget about the accident. Isn't that what friends do? Try to make you forget? We drank for hours sitting in my room. Mom and Dad didn't say anything. They were just happy I was alive and home. I could hardly sleep that night replaying the accident scene in my head asking myself, *"What could I have done differently? I should have listened to myself and gone back the next day or something."* The guilt was eating me alive and it made me so restless, playing this scene over and over again until I could hear the sounds of the impact of the car hitting us. It was a terrible thud, then the screeching sound of tires skidding and then the screams of the people who witnessed the accident as the club was closing. I can hardly forget the sounds even until this day.

THE WORST DAY EVER
SUNDAY, MARCH 13, 1983

Around 8:00 AM Sunday morning, after a restless night of replaying the scene of the accident over and over and wondering if could I have done anything differently, I called Sadye's brother, Mitch, and inquired how the girls were doing. Mitch casually replied, *"Listen, we're on our way to see you. We'll talk then."* I simply replied, *"Okay. See you then."* Well, some time had gone by and around 10:30 AM I heard the doorbell ring and I figured it had to have been Mitch. So I waited a few minutes and no one came back to see me… And a little more time passed and still no one came to see me. Now worry started to set in because it was more than a half an hour that had passed and now I'm thinking, *"Something is wrong and they're trying to figure out how to tell me. Something must be wrong…"*

A while later my bedroom door opened. In walked Michael, Mitch's roommate, Frank, and his wife, Faye, Mitch, and my mother and father. And the most dreadful feeling I had ever felt in my life came over me and I knew the way they all came in the room and circled around me it was if they knew they were about to tell me something horrible and they were placing themselves in the room to support me. All I could think was, *"Not Sadye! Not Sadye… Please not Sadye!"* Then my mother came around the bed to my right side and sat on the bed and as gently as she could say to me, *"Greg. I have some bad news. Sadye did not make it."* I just screamed and yelled out *"Ohhh No! Oh no! Not Sadye! Ohh God not her! I wanted to marry her!"* Mom embraced me to her bosom and I just cried and cried. It was the most horrible feeling of emptiness I had ever felt. I had never lost anyone so close to me, ever. I was making plans to marry her and now she was gone. What was I going to do? The unrelenting tears just kept flowing down my face.

My heart was shattered. I had no purpose. My life was lost. I could see Faye's tears as she sobbed for me knowing my loss and hers. Sadye was her best friend. No one said another word. I managed to stop crying for a bit and my friends had to leave as they had to share this devastating news to other family and friends. It was indeed, the worse day of my life and I was inconsolable. After they left, my dad came in the room and asked how I was doing. I simply replied, *"I hate this goddamn world."*

SIDE NOTE: The reason why it took everyone so long to come back to my bedroom is because Mitch was the only person I told about my feelings and plans to marry Sadye. He was trying to tell my parents how devastated I was going to be when they told me she had passed away. I never got to ask her to marry me. However, I know in my heart she would have said yes. One thing I have learned on the road called LIFE; *"Sometimes we make plans that God will not endorse. This was one of those times. I had no idea why this happened. But happened it did and there was no changing it. Death is permanent…at least for now."*

CHAPTER 14

DEPRESSION AND DRUGS

Drugs became my livelihood. I found myself in the worst hell I could think of. I did not want to live and I did not want to die. So I found myself trying to drown my sorrows in beer, liquor and drugs. Friends would bring me some of everything from weed to cocaine. It didn't matter because I was in such a place of remorse that none of it seemed to help. The alcohol just made me more depressed but that didn't seem to stop me. So for an entire week, I stayed in bed with no *"medical instructions"* to get out of bed. I had my first doctor's appointment that Friday since the accident. I tried, for the first time, to stand up Thursday afternoon, but unfortunately, my leg muscles had atrophied and they did not have the strength to hold me. I tried several times to stand up with my mother's help but unsuccessful. So that evening mom came home with a wheelchair. I was so excited because I had not been out of my room for an entire week! I loved all my Jimi Hendrix posters, but I was ready for a change of scenery!

Later that evening, Greg and Tom can back over with their usual groceries of beer and liquor. So when they arrived, to their surprise, I rolled up in the wheelchair to answer the front door. They were so happy to see me moving that they just yelled and clapped for me! It made me feel like I had hit a milestone. God was looking after me all the time, even though I was not fully acknowledging it...yet. So we drank...and we drank and I got high off coke and weed. We laughed and hung out.

Finally, Saturday evening rolled around and my brother came by and saw my state of depression and looked and said, *"Man. I haven't seen you this messed up ever."* And I realized he was right. I had never been that messed up ever over anything. So he said, *"Man you just need to get 'good and high'!"*

And I asked him, *"What do you have?"* So he asked if I had any money. I did. I asked him how much did he need. He replied, *"Do you have $100?"* So I told him he could take $100. About two hours later he came back and handed me this white folded piece of paper that felt kind of heavy. When I opened it, it had over a gram of coke in it. So I took a snort on the left and then one on the right and POWWW! That stuff went straight to my head. I couldn't believe how quickly that coke took off! I was on a sleigh ride for sure, and I had so much of it! I had never seen this much cocaine before. So I asked my brother if he could grab my guitar from the basement and bring it to me. I sat and played that guitar for hours and hours. It seemed to be my only medication. My coke and my guitar. By Monday morning, my mother asked me if I needed her to stay with me or could she go to work now. So I told her it was fine to go to work, only waiting for the moment I knew she had pulled out of the driveway and I pulled out my pipe, some weed and my coke and I mixed them together in a coke-weed cocktail and smoked it. It was long before I ever heard about free-basing or crack. But boy did it get me high.

(I am in no way condoning the use of illicit drugs in any way. However, this is the truth of my story.)

With that said, I can tell you that the drugs and my guitar saved my life. My parents and I did not know about *"counseling,"* much less Christian Counseling or help with substance abuse, because they didn't know the extent of my use or how bad it was. Whatever they knew they figured it was holding me on…and it was. But that's the catch. It was holding on to me in ways that I never imagined at the time. The addiction was holding on to me like eagle's talons and not letting me go. Like any addiction, it is chemically designed to creep into your physical body and then spread like wildfire, wreaking havoc and destruction along the way. No one ever does something that is *"highly addictive"* with the intention of getting addicted. I didn't start smoking cigarettes with the intention of getting addicted to cigarettes. I didn't start smoking marijuana with the intention of getting addicted to marijuana... And YES YOU CAN GET ADDICTED TO MARIJUANA! Contrary to popular belief. I didn't start snorting cocaine because I intended to get addicted to cocaine, nor did I eventually start smoking crack because I had a desire to get addicted to crack. I started smoking and doing drugs because of *"curiosity."* While they say, *"Curiosity killed the cat!"* It didn't seem to kill me, at least right away. With each addiction, I first would say, *"No. I'm not going to do that.".* I had a resistance to it and a strict desire *"Not to do those things!"* I had morals. I wanted to be clean.

However, you, especially parents, must know this... *"The Devil is PATIENT! And he is a LIAR!"* The things you swear you will never do become passé and ordinary in your life, if not habit. The things I vowed I would never do, soon became so habitual that I could not do without them. I just thought this was what *"adults did"* and that I was *"maturing."* Little did I know how much my maturing would cost me. It nearly cost me my life. But thank God, my Lord and my Savior was with me. The Bible says in **Hebrews 13:5** *Let your* conduct *be* without covetousness; *be* content with such things as you have. For He Himself has said, *"I will never leave you nor forsake you."* And I can tell you the TRUTH. Jesus has never ever left my side. The fact that I am writing this book is evidence of His Love and Mercy for my life and yours. Let me continue.

CHAPTER 15

RETURNING BACK TO WORK

So after about a month of recovery at home I finally returned to work. I was now fully immersed in my addiction to cocaine and seemed like I always had to have it. The one thing about drugs is; *"You always recognize another user."* And so here I was back at Channel 9 working the late shift by myself with a pocket full of coke. I would walk around the building to see if there was an empty bathroom to get a little taste. I walked into one bathroom and thought I was by myself and took a hit when I heard two guys in the same stall. I didn't know what was up. So I just left. A little while later, one of the guys, who I knew very well came to me and asked me if I wanted a hit. So I said, *"Sure. Let's hit the bathroom."* I think he wanted to make sure I wasn't going to bust him. So I took a hit of his and I could tell there was a lot of cut (watered down) on it. So I pulled out my little envelope and said, *"Yours is okay. Try this."* So he took one hit on each side and I could see his expression change! He knew I had some powerful coke and it was no joke. Yep, I just made a new friend. Everyone knows the difference between good stuff and mediocre…and mine was beyond good, it was GREAT and Tony The Tiger would say! You have to be a little older to know that one!

THE DRUG DEALER HOUSE AND THE MURAL

During my time of recovery, I sent my brother back to his contact for cocaine a couple of times and finally got to meet him in person. His name was David but everyone called him *"Chip."* He was about five-foot-six pretty short and looked kind of like the music artist, Prince. He seemed nice enough and even gave me a little extra coke after hearing about my accident. I started getting to know him and was able to go make a score on my own. One evening I was there during my evening dinner break from Channel 9 News and he was talking with some guys about refurbishing his house, which was in NW DC. While they were talking, I mentioned how he could really make the house by putting a mural in his bedroom and in the hallway. This was a big project, but he loved the idea. We both looked through several *Architectural Digest* magazines to get ideas and came up with an ancient Roman theme with coliseums, sculptures, and even a tiger painted next to his bed. It had to look like it was lying right next to the bed. Chip invested a lot of money putting up new drywall all in the rooms and hallways and he paid me in cocaine every night he'd leave me an eight ball, about $150 worth of coke then. I was more than happy to feed my addiction and express my creativity through painting every night but after about two weeks of non-stop getting high, with no sleep and turning around and going to work from 3:00 PM to 11:00 PM it got to be too much. I went home one night after work and all I could do was just crash, and I mean really crash hard. I closed my eyes and I slept so hard that if the house had blown up I would have just rolled over and snored through it.

Chip was in a hurry to make progress and have the murals finished. The problem was there were other workers in the house at the same time and they too were getting paid in powder. This was a serious problem. Once they ran out of their payment, they would come to me asking for a hit. What's worse, Sean, the guy who was supposed to be watching the workers started free-basing (smoking the cocaine) and so he really just blazed his up. And like little vampires would come upstairs where I was working and start to pressure me for coke so they could continue their madness.

Finally, instead of going to the house, I found where Chip was staying at a hotel in Virginia, just across the bridge in Crystal City. I got the address and room number from Sean and went there to report what was going on. No one was at the house to let me in and he didn't leave my usual payment. I knocked on the door and there were about five or size very beautiful ladies, which were always around him and a couple of guys waiting to score. It was late, around 11:00 PM and Chip walked in and he was definitely upset. Someone had messed up his deal so he didn't have any coke and we all were sitting there like vampires waiting to get a taste of blood, with no one to provide a taste. Chip called me into the bedroom and asked, *"What are you doing here? I thought you were working."*

"No one's at the house to let me in and I didn't have my usual supply."

"You can't work one night for me? You owe me." At that point, he grabbed a nickel-plated 45-cal. pistol off the night stand and put it in his lap. I wasn't afraid of him but accidents happen when people are upset. *"Chip, put the gun down please. There's no need for that."* Well, he was indeed upset and accused me of not making any progress on the murals. I have to admit, it would have been easier if I didn't have to contend with the other guys always trying to get my coke and interfere with my work.

Well, in a strange way, the Lord was looking out for me by sending me to see Chip and not being at the house that evening because someone had gotten in the house and stole some very expensive camera equipment. That was intolerable and someone was going to pay. The good news was, he knew I had nothing to do with it because he was my alibi and I was with him when it happened. I kept on working for a few more months on the mural until I heard that Chip had been arrested and locked up. The house had been seized by the police. I drove by the house one night after work and looked into the upper window where I was doing the mural and all my work had been painted over and whitewashed. It was all gone. No one ever got to see my work or creativity I spent so many hour/s working on. It now just lives in my memory.

CHAPTER 16

MY FIRST MARRIAGE
NOVEMBER 24, 1984

Love at first hate. Kimberly and I loved to hate one another. We were doomed together from the very beginning. It was a strange relationship because when I first met her she was out with a friend of mine who was getting married the next day and they had another friend tagging along and came to visit my buddy, Bill from around the corner. All I know is that while the three guys I was with were trying to hit on her, I was the only one who didn't and she wanted to get to know me. Somehow she got my phone number and tried to entice me to come see her since her parents were away but, I was faithful to my girlfriend at the time and did not want to mess that up. We'd talk on the phone but the fact that I was true to my girlfriend I think intrigued her even more. Kim moved away for a while and I stopped hearing from her. Two years later, she called my house and my Uncle Ralph, who happened to be in town from England, answered the phone. I don't know what she said to him but he was so *"charmed"* by her he made sure that I called her back right away. We went through a semester of back and forth until we finally broke up and she moved back to Indiana with her parents.

One evening after my car accident I called long distance to Kimberly's parents' home in Indiana. She wasn't home so I informed her mother I had been in a terrible car accident and was just recovering and asked her mom to let her know I called.

Later that evening I got a call from her and we had a long discussion about our breakup. I told her that *"If we're going to get back together, this time it's for good and asked her to marry me."* It wasn't the most romantic proposals, but she still happily accepted and I told her; *"Hey, if we're going to do this, let's do it right. Let's do it all or not at all."* So we were engaged to get married in November 1984…and we did. It was an up and down relationship filled with all kinds of drug use, mistakes, lies, and fights. After six years of a tumultuous marriage I filed for divorce and it ended in 1992. My ex moved out of the house we were renting but not before cleaning me out of house and home leaving me with a television, a VCR and a cot to sleep on. Though the material things she left me with were sparse I slept a full night of sleep for the very first time in months. I was in an empty house but my mind was clear and free.

I stayed in the house for another year until my landlord decided she was going to raise the rent to add about another $200 per month. So of course, I decided to move out to an apartment. Little did I realize… I moved right into *"Crack Central."* I moved miles away from my old place of residence right off of New Hampshire Avenue, just across the DC line. Some of you know exactly where I am talking about. So I just had finished moving in and had some errands to run and driving down the street I saw a guy, Leonard, sitting on a wall and I knew this guy knew where to get some crack. I just asked him outright; *"You got any rock?"*

"Yeah. How much you want?"

"I'll be back in a bit and get back to you." When I came back he was still sitting on the wall and he approached my car, a BMW 325i. I got a $20 hit from him and went back to my apartment. I remember how this all started with Leonard. Little did I know, I truly was dealing with one of Satan's Little Helpers. This guy was as devious as they come. He was evil and methodical and would learn every little detail about you so he could run his scams on you.

After about a year of meeting different drug dealers in the neighborhood, Leonard got jealous of me...who knows why. I had and he didn't. ***The Haves and the Have-Nots***, I suppose. So one day, Leonard plotted to rob me and kept calling me and asking me if *"so-n-so"* was there, to which I replied; *"Nope. Haven't seen him."*

CHAPTER 17

SEPTEMBER 1994:
A KNOCK ON THE DOOR

Later that evening, about 10:30 PM someone buzzed the front door and used the same name Leonard had been asking for earlier that day. So I buzzed the guy in. A few minutes later I heard a knock and, assuming it was this guy Leonard had been looking for, I opened the door. There in front of me were three unfamiliar faces and a 9mm pistol that was familiar, pointing in my chest. I recognized the gun. It was the exact same gun Leonard had shown me a week before, I looked and told the guys; *"C'mon, man! I don't have anything."*

"You know wuts up." And the guy with gun grabbed me in the chest by my shirt and pulled me into the hallway. My heart was racing like never before. I didn't know how serious these guys were and if they were going to shoot me or not. All I knew is that I could be dead any second. They walked me down the hall to the elevator which seemed like the longest walk of my life. As we got to the elevator, the guy with the gun walked in front of me with the gun to his side. The other two were behind me. I knew I had to do something but what? Then out of nowhere I remembered some martial arts training and remembered the words of Bruce Lee; *"When your opponent takes his eyes off of you attack."* And so I did! I reached over the shoulders of the guy with the gun and wrapped my hands around his hands and the gun. I had a very tight grip on

his hands and gun and he could not get out of it. Then I started yelling out to my neighbors; *"They have a gun and they are trying to shoot me! Call the police!"* Well with that, the other two guys took off and I was left wrestling with this guy for the gun. We tussled and struggled until we fell against the wall and slid down to the floor. I had such a tight grip that I held on to his hands and the gun all the way. Meanwhile, the biggest of the guys came back and his friend tried to slide the gun to him on the floor.

GUARDIAN ANGEL

For He Himself has said, *"I will never leave you nor forsake you."* (**Hebrews 5:13, NKJV**)

Now I don't know his name, but I do know that my guardian angel was there with me that night because, when the guy tried to slide the gun to other guy standing over top of me, who had the advantage over me, he could not take the gun, even though I only had a *"loose grip"* of the handle of the gun. So the big guy punched me in that back of my head and I literally saw stars like you see in cartoons. Then he kicked me in my spine and I knew I had to end this quickly or I could end up dead. Somehow (guardian angel) I lifted up off the floor still holing this guy's hands clinched in mine with the gun still tussling over it. Finally, the gun fired off and the other guy ran out of the building and I got away while the guy ran after his buddies saying; *"Man! We had him! Y'all let him get away!"* I ran back down my hallway and back into my apartment huffing and puffing and out of breath. I had just fought for my life not realizing how close I really may have been to death.

A little while later, my phone rang. It was the signal. If there was no answer, the coast was clear. My home was empty and he could clean me out. If I answered, though, he knew they messed up. Well, we know that I answered. I told him I knew it was him, though he denied it. But he knew his boys blew it. After all, I was a punk. I was a crack head. There was no way I could fight my way out with three guys there. And the truth is… I didn't. Without my guardian angel. (Thank you very much!) I would not be writing this story today. Never under estimate what God will do in your life through your angel who has been assigned to you…whether you believe or not. What I do know, most definitively, is that; God has spared my life on more than one occasion and probably more than I know or can count. But I know for certain…that night God, once again, spared my life…literally.

A few weeks later, I sat down with Leonard and right after he had taken a huge puff off his pipe, I told him; *"I know it was you. I know you're the one who set me up."*

"Naww, man. If I was gonna hit you, I'dah dunnit myself."

"You don't have the guts to come after me yourself. That's why you sent those boys over here and they didn't get the job done. Don't send a boy to do a man's job son!"

"How do you know it was me?"

"Because I recognized your gun. You forgot that I saw it just the week before. I recognized that "square slide over the barrel" you had. I have a very good memory."

Leonard continued to be Leonard as I got deeper into crack addiction.

It had been two years that I lived in that neighborhood in my apartment, just up the street from my brother, Steve, who was very well known in the political arena in Washington, DC. He was most successful in his career with a six-figure salary and company car. One night around 10:30 PM, he was driving past my apartment and called me. *"Hey, man, wuts up? Do you know where I can get some coke?"*

"Yep. C'mon by." He was at my apartment in just a few minutes and we took a ride up the street. He gave me a crisp $100 bill right out the ATM. He told me to get $50 of powder and $50 of crack for me. No problem! I scored the stuff in just a few minutes and got back in the car. We went to my apartment and he sniffed and I blazed up. We were quite the team. He had the money and I had the time and the connection to some good stuff.

So the next evening, he came by with the same request. Fifty-fifty order and no problem. We got to my apartment and while he was taking a sniff made the comment, *"Man, I wish there was a way I could do the coke and not get my nose all bluffed up. My wife catches me every time."* So I replied while taking a hit of crack, *"Man, I hit this crack and there's no residual, only high and people can't tell because there's no powder marks on your nose and face."*

Famous Last Words: So I asked my brother, *"You wanna try it?"* He hesitated for a second or so and then said, *"Okay."* So I handed my brother the pipe and gave him the hit that would change his life for the next several years. I had no idea of the devastation crack would cause my brother and to this day I regret ever even saying the words, much less actually handing him the pipe. When he took his very first hit of crack I saw instantly his eyes got big and I could see the rush hit his brain and he just said, *"WOWWW! That was intense!"* So he took another hit, rode the wave for a bit and then went home.

The very next morning, my brother called me at 10:00 AM saying he was stopping by and just around the corner. I looked out my fourth floor window only to see him strolling across the parking lot in a t-shirt, shorts and his briefcase. I thought to myself, *"Dude! What's going on?"* So when he got to my door I buzzed him in and when he got inside the apartment, I asked him what was up. *"Man, call your boy. I want to get some more."*

"Don't you have to go to work?"

"Naaah, I cancelled my appointments for today."

"Seriously? Dude, it can wait."

So I was trying to understand the *"urgency."* It'll be here later. Go to work. Right? However, little did I know that those *"crack talons"* had already lunged inside of my brother and had taken over. The reason why I even gave my brother that hit was because ***"I NEVER SAW ANYONE GET ADDICTED SO FAST AND INSTANTLY"*** like it hit my brother. In all the years I did drugs, I never stayed home from work to get high. I always went to work and all of my friends who got high went to work. Getting high is what I did during and after work as did many of my friends. I didn't know anyone who didn't go to work because they stayed home just to get high. However, little did we know about my brother's bipolar disorder and probably other issues. Let me just say for the record, my brother Steve is clean now and has been for over fifteen years and resumed working in local government and raising millions of dollars for his organization and is at the top of his game! He is a real inspiration to many who saw his downfall and comeback and an inspiration to me.

After a couple of years of the struggles with crack cocaine, I realized that I needed to stop and the voice of the Holy Spirit was speaking to me. I believe the Holy Spirit speaks to us all, every day. The problem is, we don't hear His Voice. Why, you ask? Our Father in Heaven has been trying to reach each and every one of us that we might receive His Gift of Salvation through the Death and Resurrection of Jesus Christ, our Lord.

Meanwhile, during all this drama, my girlfriend, now wife, Minerva, had been ministering to me in a very kind and loving way. She was then, and always had been my best friend. She and I started talking about church and things and explained how involved she was at church. Well I didn't understand. *"What's there to get involved with? Don't you just go and then leave, like we do in the Catholic Church?"* She explained how close she was with the pastor and his wife and how she was on different committees. So one day I said to her, *"Do you think we could go to church together? It might be good for your son to see us going to church together."*

CHAPTER 18

CHURCH VISIT: CAPITOL HILL SDA CHURCH

So one weekend, my wife's cousin came in town and wanted to visit a Seventh-day Adventist Church in Washington, DC, as they were both Seventh-day Adventists. So we attended their Bible Study or *"Sabbath School Lesson Study"* and then listened to a most beautiful song service. Finally, when Pastor John Nixon came up to preach, it was like the Holy Spirit was speaking right through him to me. I was amazed and truly taken by his words. I have never heard a priest speak at a Catholic service like this! This was something special! We were at church for more than two hours and I wanted more! I couldn't believe it with my Catholic background.

When church was over, we stepped outside and I stood right in front of the doors saying, *"I can't believe it! We've been here over two hours and I want to hear more!" I've never been in church this long and wanted more!"* Little did I know, but I was being fed and lead by the Holy Spirit! This was God's Work and it was WORKING! So I told them, *"We're gonna have to come back next week and bring your mother, your sister and her kids! This was amazing!"* So the following Saturday, we did just that. My girlfriend, her mother, her sister, her nieces and her son and I took up an entire row! And just as before, Pastor John Nixon, preached the Word of God and my heart was moved even more! However, at the end of his sermon, Pastor Nixon made this statement, *"There's someone sitting here right now who needs to give their life to Christ. If that's you, just raise your hand."* And immediately my hand went up! I don't even know if it was me that actually raised it, but up it went. A deaconess came to me with a card and I filled it out.

That following Monday, I got a phone call from the pastor, and he asked, *"Hello, this is Pastor John Nixon, what can I do for you?"*

"Well, Pastor, I was at your service on Saturday and I liked what I heard. Maybe I can get in Bible study or something."

He then asked, *"Can you get here this Saturday at 9:30 AM?"*

"Yes, I can." Minerva and I were there at 9:00 AM waiting for the doors to open! This started my journey into Bible studies and getting prepared for baptism. She attended every class with me, just in case I had any questions or concerns she could answer. That was in June of 1997.

By August it was announced that Pastor Nixon was leaving the Capitol Hill SDA Church to move to Oakwood University in Huntsville, Alabama and his last day would be September 20, 1997. So the group of us that were in Bible studies got baptized that day. All in all, there were seven of us who gave their lives to Christ that day.

SEPTEMBER 20, 1997: MY BAPTISM

I remember getting prepared for my baptism and writing a statement about myself and how Jesus Christ came into my life. I invited my parents to attend the service even though they were devoted Catholics, they dressed their best, as always, and attended my baptism into the Seventh-day Adventist Church on Capitol Hill. Of course, mom told me she couldn't stay afterward because she had a most-important card game with her girlfriends that afternoon. I was so thankful that she attended all the same. Mom and Dad were very supportive of all their kids in any way they could be.

CHAPTER 19

AFTER BAPTISM TRIALS

Well, if you have never been baptized, let me share this with you... *"Get prepared for the real trials!"* I say this because *"We are ALL SINNERS in need of God's Mercy and Jesus's Death and Resurrection that provides the FREE GIFT of Salvation."* So know this, that at the time of my baptism, I was still smoking crack, still smoking cigarettes and drinking alcohol. And while the Seventh-day Church, as many others teach against such things, we did not discuss it much during my Bible studies. No fault of the church. However, I was not prepared to just give up these things immediately. But I fought a good battle...for a while.

Right after my baptism, a pastor, Leo Schreven, was visiting Takoma Academy, an SDA school, from out of town to do a presentation on the Books of Daniel and Revelation for six days a week for a month.

Boy, oh boy was this the most powerful and influential series I have ever studied on this subject! So here I was in Bible Studies for a couple of months got baptized, and a week later, I'm in the midst of the most intense Bible Studies ever with Leo Schreven, who was a renowned teacher on this topic. I learned the different Books of the Bible and where to find certain topics and really was immersed in the Word of God, and attending this series with Minerva and her mother! AMEN!

So after Leo Schreven left town, she and I went through with-drawal because we didn't know what to do with our evenings now that we had this free time. So a couple, Gary and Ann, that we met at the series had borrowed the entire VHS series of Leo Schreven's videotapes to record them. There were twenty-four tapes in all. So they gave us half the tapes to record and when done, gave us the other half. So we got to go through the entire series again. During this time I managed to stay away from the drugs and the crack and the people involved in it... In fact, all during the year I had a part-time job as an intern at WETA Channel 26 doing news graphics for the News Hour with Jim Leher. I was paid pretty well for an intern position but it still wasn't full-time employment. However, sometimes you have to take what you can get to get what you want. I really liked the Art Department team and the art director, Calvin and I got along very well and he understood that I needed work. So he brought me in and allowed me to work as long as I needed until something better came along. And boy, did the Lord bless me indeed. Less than a month after I was baptized and after study-ing with Leo's seminars, I got a job offer for a full-time position I had applied for some time ago. I started in mid-October 1997 at Chesapeake Directory Sales designing Yellow Page advertise-ments. I worked there for over seventeen years. God had blessed me... And He spared me because during my employment there were several mergers which, oftentimes would cause the company to let employees go or RIF them and I managed to stay on to the very end, until the company outsourced all our graphic design work to India.

CHAPTER 20

THE TRIALS

Just know this… Even though I had given my life to the Lord and was baptized, I was still smoking cigarettes and drinking. While I managed to stop smoking crack cocaine for a short while, the desires were still there. I had not fully surrendered all of my addictions to Jesus and hence, I was struggling this battle on my own. Some of you reading this, especially Christians, who have never dealt with addiction, serious addictions, probably cannot relate at all to what I am saying. A person who's never driven over 55mph can't understand what it's like to drive 150mph. They can't understand the sensation. To those who have never taken drugs or alcohol, they have no reference why people do it."

Sorry, they just don't get it.

THE DESIRE OF ADDICTION CAME BACK

And then it came back, the desire. The craving for drugs hit me again. I was so new and fresh in my *New Life in Christ* that I had no idea of the dangers of old habits returning and overcoming me. So I drove back to my old neighborhood and stopped at Leonard's to see if I could buy a $20 hit. But he noticed there was something different about me and I told him I had been baptized in the church. He looked at me a bit strangely but sold me the bag all the same.

Here is where the downward spiral started again. I had never dealt with my addiction to crack or other addictions. Each one was its own vice all by itself and they all had to be dealt with differently. For three more years, I was doing drugs and smoking and being able to hide the use from my girlfriend and my parents...or so I thought.

Meanwhile, my brother's addiction to crack had grown astronomically! He was stopping by daily, sometimes in the morning, sometimes in the afternoon but definitely in the evening. We had a variety of dealers would come by and sell just about everything they had to us while we sat and played backgammon through the night. However, this all came crashing down on me one day when some guys stopped by my apartment to get money from my brother who wasn't there. He gave me some money to pay one guy and three or four showed up because he promised the same money to three other people. One guy was high or drunk, or both and got indignant with me demanding his money. He started getting louder and louder in my apartment and then picked up a set of wooden knunchakas (knum chucks) I had and started swinging them to try to use them. As he started to get louder I told him he had to leave and grabbed him, threw him up against the door and grabbed the knunchakas. With one swift move, I took them and then wrapped one of his arms crossed inside them and then twisted his arm in them! In other words, I could have easily broken his arm...and believe me, I was trying to! I saw his eyes pop when I applied the pressure and he was helpless. Right when I was about to throw him out of the apartment, I was jumped from behind and pulled to the floor by one of the other guys and pinned down. He raised his fist over my face and said, *"Don't make me do it, Greg! Don't make me do it man! Don't make me do it!"* I looked right into his face and told him he better get off me or he was going to pay! The guys finally left after suspecting someone was going to call the police because of the noise. I knew then, once again, *"You can trust no one."* Anyone, no matter what you do for them, will turn on you in an instant. I went through many years of addictions of all types: cigarettes, alcohol and various illegal drugs, like marijuana, speed, cocaine and crack.

CHAPTER 21

HIDING MY ADDICTIONS: NO ONE KNOWS

Ever since I was a teenager and started smoking I was able to hide the packs of cigarettes for a while. When you live with parents that smoke, it wasn't too hard. Later, as I got into doing drugs, I got good at *"Hiding my addictions and paraphernalia"* to the point that I believe I went years without my parents knowing. However, there always comes a point that the *"Things are in darkness will come to light"* and they always did. I was even able to hide, for the most part, my serious addictions from my girlfriend, now wife. Let me be clear, my wife, Minerva, **NEVER DID DRUGS!** I never did drugs around her and she NEVER EVER saw me do drugs. She saw me on occasion when I was high, but may not have even known then. It wasn't until both my brother and I grenaded our lives in front of our parents did the truth come to light that we were crack addicts. When she found out it was the most horrible day of my life because I had to admit to my addiction and now claim to get the help I needed.

I went on for a while feigning to be clean and sober, but again, I knew how to hide and cover up and make excuses for certain behavior. But the truth is, I was still very much addicted to drugs and cigarettes and alcohol. However, that did not stop me from loving my girlfriend whom I wanted to marry. We had known each other from our teenage years and it was indeed a dream of hers from early on.

CHAPTER 22

OUR WEDDING DAY
APRIL 11, 1999

In the spring of 1999 I planned to marry the love of my life, Minerva. We decided to do a *"musical"* theme because we just loved jazz music and listening to music and dancing in her parents' basement was part of our history. We loved to sing, dance and talk until her dad would say, *"Minerva, do you know what time it is?"* Well, now after all those years of friendship we would now become husband and wife. Well we had planned a very lovely ceremony with flowers that my fiancé designed for the wedding and draped the archway where we were to stand. Wednesday prior to the wedding our pastor, Patrick, baptized us together in preparation for our union together. It was a special moment and we had just immediate family there to witness it. I remember Minerva's, niece, Teresa, who was about fifteen years old, came to me at the side door of the church and gave me her *"family warning"* and said, *"Don't hurt Minerva. Okay?"* So I could do nothing but comply. It was a warning not to be taken lightly and I knew it.

On Sunday, April 11, 1999, my wife's son from her previous marriage, Nicholas, walked my bride down the aisle. We all felt that, since we were becoming a family of three it should be her son who gives her to me. It was indeed a very special moment for us. I will not bore you with the details of how the limousine that my best man and his wife paid for to pick up my bride and her bridesmaids at our apartment got into an accident on the way to pick them up. And I certainly won't bore you on how I had to run interference between them and the limousine company because the girls were in an uproar. And if that wasn't enough, I really won't bore you with the details of the limo company hiring another driver to pick them up and was over an hour late. And meanwhile, I was in the back preparation room in the church waiting the entire time for my bride and the dear sweet organist, Marilyn Petersen, now deceased, played ever so sweetly the entire time and no one seemed to notice a thing. But I won't bore you with that.

Now that we had been married for a time, I started going back to my old tricks of getting high, because the fact is, I never really *stopped.* It was more like a pause. I can tell you from experience, that crack cocaine and some of these other drugs nowadays are so potent that people become *"fully addicted"* and taken in by the Satanic forces almost immediately. Many of you have no idea of what I am referring to, but for those of you who do, you know exactly what I mean. Here's something else you need to know. There are many *"functioning addicts"* out there that, like me, who would go to work, come home, play mom or dad and still find a way to get high and for the most part, people may not know. You may see some visible signs that you've ignored, such as: extended stays in the bathroom, out in the garage way too long looking for nothing, or visiting a friend you know they have no business being around. However, the bottom line is: If someone you love is an addict, of any type, you must get them help, especially if they're using harsher drugs and chemicals to get high. ***IT IS AN EPIDEMIC THAT YOU CANNOT OUTSPEND!*** As the saying goes, *"One's too many and a thousand is not enough."* Parents especially. Do not think you can pay off your kids drug debts and think they will stop. This is a *"Tough Love Battle"* and if you want to win then you have to be tough…and yes, *"It is indeed TOUGH!"* However, if you hang in there with them and share with them the love that you have them and the love that Christ has for them, you *"May win this battle. No promises."* It is a *"Fight To The Finish."*

However, know this too, *"It can be done and the battle can be won! Don't give up—EVER!"* As long as there is breath in you and your loved one, *"Don't give up!"* By the same token, *"Don't give in! That does more harm than good and only prolongs addictions,"* sometimes for years and years.

However, through all this, I really hit a turning point. While I was still sneaking around whenever I could to get high, I was still reading my Bible and studying my Sabbath School Lessons faithfully, and for the most part, I could tell they were having an effect because the Holy Spirit was indeed reaching me and I could not fight the Holy Spirit. He was the One who first moved in me to take that first step toward Christianity, and now, He was leading me again back down the path of righteousness. The Holy Spirit was tugging on my heart all the while. That's when you know that the Spirit is moving in your life. You question the things you're doing and question whether it is *"right or wrong"* and your heart knows that you cannot continue on the path you're on.

Well, back in October of 1999, we had open enrollment for our Health Care at my job and I put down that I was not a smoker because I knew I wanted to quit but also thought I could save some money. After having a conversation with a co-worker who told me, *"Well, you know if you don't quit and then you get a related disease, the insurance won't cover you."* Well, that was enough for me. So I quit smoking cigarettes in January 2000. It was the beginning of my journey of overcoming my addictions once and for all. Cigarettes seemed easy after the first week or so. I prayed to God and asked Him to help me and He did. Cold turkey! No patch or gum and especially, no brainwashing that I needed another drug to help me quit another drug so I could develop another addiction and cause more problems. And then things changed for me again.

Well, here's another caveat. You may have heard the saying, *"Be careful for what you ask for."* Well, after a couple of years going by, I realized that the more I read the Bible the more I realized I needed to read the Bible more, and I am a terribly slow reader, PERIOD! However, I knew that I had to get over this. But can I say this? God is AMAZING! He knew my heart and knew my request.

CHAPTER 23

JANUARY 2000:
"WOULD YOU DO ME A FAVOR?"

So one Saturday morning at the end of Sabbath School Lesson Study, the teacher, Michael Herron, asked me if I would do him a favor for next Sabbath. *"Would you teach Sabbath School next week?"* I was so shocked by the idea and I replied, *"Well, before I answer, can you tell me why you picked me? I'm the newest member in here!"* And he replied, *"Well, it wasn't me but my dear lovely wife, Gwendolyn, who happened to notice your lesson book was filled with all kinds of notes and highlights. So we at least knew you were reading the lessons!"* Well, I accepted but I was still very nervous about this daunting task. So you know that thing I was talking about how slow I read. Well here was God's answer. *"Okay, my son, you need to read? Here, I'll let you teach! Then you'll have to read!"*

I had never taught anything and here I was going to teach something from the Bible no less! As always, I prayed about this and then during the week I met with Michael, at his home to review my notes. He sat with me and carefully reviewed everything and thought I would do just fine. Saturday/Sabbath morning came and my wife and I went to church and boy I was ready! I taught my first Sabbath School Lesson Study and LOVED IT! The class was engaged and answering questions and I realized, I had found my niche. Evidently, the next day several people called Michael, and informed him how I did. Later in the week I saw him at a

Revelation series with Ron Halverson, who wrote a book entitled, *"Prayer Warriors."* After the presentation was done, Michael came to me and said he had gotten some very nice compliments on my teaching that past Sabbath and asked if I would like to teach again this week. I was absolutely ecstatic and told him that I would love to teach again! I have been teaching ever since and never looked back.

CHAPTER 24

MY FINAL BOUT WITH DRUGS

It was a Thursday evening in late spring of 2000 and it was the day before payday and I decided to get high. I first stopped at a friend's house and smoked a couple of hits in their kitchen and after running out of crack decided to leave and head home around 11:30 PM. However, I wouldn't get to my homeward destination after taking a bad turn and detoured back in my old neighborhood, crack central. It was just after midnight and my direct deposit had gone through so I had plenty of cash to work with. The hours passed like minutes, I had burned through the crack like a hot knife, and now dawn was breaking and it was almost time for me to go to work. I had not been home all night. I didn't call home and my ATM would not dispense any more money because I had run my limit for the day. It was 7:00 AM and I was out of money and the drug dealer was like, *"Man…sorry, bro, but you got to go. Hit me up later when you can get some more money."* Meanwhile, my wife and my parents had found my car two doors up and was waiting for me at first. Then, my wife took the extra keys to the car and left me stranded. My parents followed her back to their house. I knew I was in deep trouble now! Everything had come to an exploding end and now I had no money, no car and not even my ATM card. The dealer kept my card as collateral until I paid him for the drugs he fronted me during the night.

DAYLIGHT AND THE
WALK OF SHAME

Well, some time had passed, there were no more drugs to be had and no one else was around and now it was time to go home and face the music. This was not a pretty song either, as I knew that facing my parents and my wife was going to be a sorrow-filled song and a slow, very slow dance. It was about a mile to the nearest gas station where they had an actual working phone booth! Some of you reading this have no idea what I'm referring to. For those of you too young to know what that is; you see, there was actually a time when people didn't walk around with cell phones, especially with cameras and all kinds of apps, etc. We actually had *"public phones in public for one use and one use only…to make a phone call."* That's it! And no, you did not take it with you. You would actually have to put a quarter in, it used to be a dime, but put a quarter in and make the phone call. If you did not have a coin you could make a *"collect phone call"* in which you would dial "0" for an *"operator"* who could then call the number you were trying to reach and then say to the receiving end, *"I have a phone call from Gregory, will you accept?"* And hopefully someone would say *"yes"* and accept the phone call.

I called my parents' house about 4:00 or 5:00 PM and told my mother where I was so she could meet me. But the most embarrassing part of all was telling her I owed a guy $70 and could she bring it so I could get my credit card back. Well my mother came to my rescue and picked me up, took me back to the neighborhood and I paid the guy off to get my ATM card back. I felt so ashamed. But the worst was yet to come, facing my wife. However, I couldn't do it. I was not ready to face that shame and guilt. We got back to my parents' home and I went into my old bedroom and shut the door. I got on my knees and with tears running down my eyes I said this prayer: *"Dear Jesus, I am so sorry. I know I need to quit the drugs. The problem is, I don't want to. I like getting high. I like doing drugs. However, I know I need to quit. So I'm asking you to "take the taste away from me" and if you do, I know I can quit doing drugs. But if you don't, I will be back doing drugs tomorrow."* Let me tell you friends, Jesus Christ did not let me down! AMEN! Jesus took that taste for drugs, for alcohol, and every addiction out of my heart and cleansed me! *JESUS CHRIST SAVED MY LIFE!* He cleansed me of my unrighteousness and made me brand new! AMEN! This is what He does and only He can do. I could have stopped doing drugs but still not be *"Righteous In The Eyes Of Our Father In Heaven!"* I can stop doing drugs, alcohol and ciga-rettes, but it does not *"make me brand-new!"*

"ONLY JESUS CHRIST CAN CLEANSE YOU OF SIN AND MAKE YOU RIGHT BEFORE OUR FATHER IN HEAVEN."

Let me just say this too. The battle for addiction still goes on but I have won the fight. I have not had drugs in over nineteen years now and I thank God for everyday and every moment I am **FREE of ADDICTION! AMEN!**

I had to eventually face my wife and that was the hardest thing I had to do in all this because she did not deserve the things that I had done. I told her when I saw her that I would get the help that I needed, even it if meant going to rehab and getting a fresh per-spective. Here is the thing: *"I never went to rehab. I prayed to God, in Jesus Christ every day and He overcame EVERY ADDICTION for me. I didn't use any patch, gum or other addictive medications to overcome my drug problem. I overcame all my addictions through prayer and Bible study. PERIOD!"*

Please know: I am in no way saying that if someone needs assis-tance to overcome their addictions to drugs, cigarettes or alcohol, not to take it. **NO ABSOLUTELY NOT.** If you need additional assistance during your rehabilitation, then by all means do so. I am only stating that I did not.

CHAPTER 25

A NOTE TO PEOPLE GOING TO AA

Let me tell you something. I do not believe alcoholism is a *"Disease"* as stated by AA and other medical industries. And here's why: AA tells you, *"Once an alcoholic, ALWAYS an alcoholic. Once an addict, ALWAYS an addict."* So essentially, AA says, *"You have a disease that has no cure… EVER!"*

"And I don't believe that! Don't let ANYONE tell you, you have a disease that can't be cured." Now I'm going to get *"scriptural"* on you.

When I prayed to Jesus to heal me of my sickness and my addictions it was not different than anyone else asking Jesus to heal them in His day. Watch this!

JESUS CLEANSES A LEPER

[8] When He had come down from the mountain, great multitudes followed Him. [2] And behold, a leper came and worshiped Him, saying, *"Lord, if You are willing, You can make me clean."*

[3] Then Jesus put out *His* hand and touched him, saying, *"I am willing; be cleansed."* Immediately his leprosy was cleansed. [4] And Jesus said to him, *"See that you tell no one; but go your way, show yourself*

to the priest, and offer the gift that Moses commanded, as a testimony to them." (**Matthew 8, NKJV**)

Case and point: Leprosy was an *"incurable disease"* in Jesus' day and yet Jesus touched the man and he was healed. So if the man who was now cleaned of leprosy, does he have to walk down the street claiming to be *"an unclean leper"*? NO. Why? Because Jesus Christ, our Lord healed him of the leprosy.

So when people call on the name of Jesus and they are healed, they can walk in their newness of life! *"Don't let anyone categorize you by a so-called disease!"* And don't let people convince you *"That you can never be healed."* Be well by the Blood of Jesus! How can alcoholism, which is basically *"self-inflicted"* be a disease? Cancer is a disease. Syphilis is a disease. Parkinson's is a disease, but not alcoholism. And it can be cured. Look at it this way: *"If you told yourself every morning when you woke up, "I feel sick." Do you believe after a month of telling yourself that, that you would get sick?"* Of course you would. *YOU MANIFEST WHAT YOU TELL YOURSELF! IT IS AS YOU BELIEVE!*

So, friends, believe that no matter what sickness you have, no matter what addictions you're suffering with, that God through the Power of the Holy Spirit in Christ Jesus, you can be healed. Amen? AMEN. More proof to come!

So a few years had gone by and I was clean! AMEN! I was so happy because I was teaching the Sabbath School Lesson Studies which were really helping me to learn and understand the Bible even more. I'm sharing the Word of God with people and it was exciting. But let me tell you something… *"Even though God cleansed me of my addictions, there was still a price to pay for all those years of smoking and drinking and the toll it took on my body."* I smoked a pack to a pack and a half a day, depending on what I was doing. You can't do that for thirty years and not expect to pay a price. And I did…

CHAPTER 26

NOVEMBER 2005:
SOMETHING IS WRONG

I started getting these strange pains in my throat when I ate. I went to my doctor, he gave me some antibiotics, but nothing. I went back to my doctor and he sent me to an ENT (Ear, Nose, and Throat) doctor in his building. She put a long scope up my nose and into my throat and it was very uncomfortable. In the end she said, *"Well, I don't see any cancer."* Months went by and every time I sat down to eat the instant I swallowed, I knew something was wrong. On at least two more occasions, I got up from the dinner table and went to the emergency room, only to get the same answer, *"We don't see anything."* However, whatever was causing the pain was getting bigger and now the pain was so severe that I had to stick my finger in my ear just to chew my food. Convinced that it now may be TMJ disorder (temporomandibular joint disorder), I went to my dear friend and dentist, Dr. Hank. I met Dr. Hank a few years before when my former dentist retired. I told Dr. Hank that I had a very *"bad"* experience with a dentist as a child and had more fear than most. He assured me that everything would be okay and that he would take good care of me. So I asked *"Doc"* as I sometimes call him, if he would examine me for TMJ. So he examined me but could not find anything that would suggest that I had temporomandibular joint disorder.

I left my friend's office feeling discouraged that I had no answers and no idea what was causing this pain, that was not only there but very real. While waiting for the elevator I saw on the wall *"ENT specialists"* next to a door across the hall. So I walked in and simply showed them my medical insurance card and said, *"Do you take this insurance?"*

"We do."

"Good, because I have a problem no one can find and you may be my last hope." So I met with Dr. Hauk, I told him how I had been to several doctors and even my dentist, but no one could find what was wrong with me. After an initial X-ray, Dr. Hauk told me, *"I know there is something wrong with you because you would not be going through all this trouble for nothing."* I felt so relieved to know I was in the right place.

Concerned that there was a serious problem unseen problem the doctor sent me to get an MRI (magnetic resonance imaging), that shows *"everything"*! When the results came back Dr. Hauk said these words, *"I can see there is a mass here in the film, but I just cannot find it on you!"* Then he took a pair of rubber gloves, put them on and reached in my throat. *"I found it! I can feel the mass!"* I could feel the mass as he pressed on it. I asked him if it was cancer and he told me he did not know and that they would have to do a biopsy. Unfortunately, it was a Friday afternoon and he was leaving for vacation that Monday morning. Dr. Hauk went in the hallway and met with one of his partners where he informed him of my situation. I could sense the seriousness of the conversation but could not hear exactly what was said. The two came in and I was introduced to Dr. Brian who would be taking over the biopsy and any other follow-up procedures. The biopsy was scheduled for that coming Wednesday. They were wasting no time!

CHAPTER 27

APRIL 2006:
"HONEY, YOU HAVE CANCER"

Wednesday, April 12, 2006, came and we did the biopsy. Dr. Brian told us it would be a few days to a week before the results came in but he ran them STAT, which means *"immediately,"* but we didn't know. So around 4:00 PM the next day I was on my way to a client's office when my wife called me. *"Honey, you need to come home right away."*

"What's wrong?" I could tell by the sound of her voice that something serious was going on. *"I don't want to tell you over the phone."*

"Well now you really have me curious. What's going on?"

"Well the doctor called." And there was a pause…

I said to her, *"Well, whatever he told you the answer isn't going to change by the time I come home. Just tell me."*

"You have cancer."

Without missing a beat I said to her, *"You're not worried, are you? We are people of faith and now we're going to walk by that faith. And where ever it takes us, I promise you, I am not dying of cancer! Not now or any time soon."*

This was the beginning of a long and very tough uphill battle. For anyone who has dealt with cancer and the treatment you know exactly what I am talking about.

So Minerva and I went to Dr. Brian's that Friday for a consultation to see what the next steps were. We were clueless. We had no idea whether we would have to travel to Philadelphia or Chicago for special treatment. So we just prayed and asked our Lord and Savior, Jesus Christ to spare me and save me. Thankfully, my doctor was on the ball and God answered our prayers. He called a local company to do a complete body and PET scan (positron emission tomography). It just so happens that the young lady, Veronica, who answered the phone to set up the appointment recognized my name, as we attend the same church. My wife overheard the conversation with the doctor and told me Veronica will be there with you! God is amazing.

Dr. Brian had set up appointments for us to meet all of the doctors involved in my treatment for the following Monday. Amazingly, and according to God's plan, all of the doctors were within a *"five-mile radius"*! We didn't know if we would have to travel out of state but God saw to it that we would be able to manage all of the treatment in one area. You may have heard the term, *"God is good. All the time. All the time, God is good."* I am here to tell you, it is the *"ABSOLUTE TRUTH"*!

On Monday, April 17, 2006, Minerva and I went to meet the oncologists, Dr. Clarke and Dr. Modin. Both doctors sat with us and started to paint this very serious and very tough journey ahead. Neither doctor painted a picture of victory, but this did not discourage us. When we met with the chemotherapist, Dr. Aylesworth, she introduced me to the nurse who would administer the actual treatments. The nurse was very lively but she told us, *"You're in for a beat down. It's not going to be pretty."* Minerva and I were not discouraged though. After all, what did we know "really" about what the treatment would do?

When we arrived home, Minerva got on the computer and started doing research on my particular form of cancer, *"squamous cell carcinoma"* and treatments for it which included radiation, chemotherapy, and *"brachytherapy,"* which is treatment with catheter implants under the chin (see diagram). By the time we had our next meeting with the doctors Minerva had done so much research that she almost anticipated what they were going to tell us. I, on the other hand seemed to be content to let things happen as they would. Maybe that was my way of just dealing with it. The less I knew about the real details the better. I was just going to face cancer head on. *"Cancer isn't killing me. I'm killing it!"* I also can tell you one thing. My boss, Paul, was the best boss ever during this whole ordeal. When I first found out that I had cancer, he immediately went to his boss and informed her. She told him to tell me, *"Go and get better. Get your treatment and get well. And don't worry...your job will be waiting for you when you get done."* When Paul came to my desk and told me that I almost broke down and cried. I had never experienced that kind of care on a job before and I knew this was serious because my life was on the line.

CHAPTER 28

CANCER: THE TREATMENT

Before I started treatment the doctors had me get a *"PEG"* Percutaneous Endoscopic Gastrostomy feeding tube inserted in my abdomen because though the surgery implant is simple, they thought it would be too much for me once I really needed it. Chemotherapy started the second week in May. Since there is no specific planning that needs to be done with chemo I started almost immediately. I noticed the very next day that the pain that I had in my inner ear when I ate and swallowed was gone! God is so good. I thought to myself, *"Boy! This is going to be a breeze if it's like this."* Little did I know I was in for the most grueling pain I could ever imagine and it wasn't going to be a roller coaster ride. This was going to be a full steam engine train coming right at me and there was nothing I could do about it but sit and take it.

So the next week I had chemotherapy again and then went home, and then back to work the next day. Finally, about two weeks later, in the middle of May 2006, I started the radiation treatment. The team of people was very special. They all knew I was about to go through living hell and yet they just kept smiling and had on their game face every day and they did the work they had to do. I have a lot of love and respect for these people who save others' lives daily. Unfortunately, not everyone makes it.

I remember a woman, Margie, sitting in the waiting room around my second radiation treatment. And for the record, radiation treatment uses *"real radiation."* It's no joke. By two thirds of the way into my treatment I had third degree burns wrapped around my face, ear to ear and my flesh was burnt from the outside all the way to the inside and everything hurt. So when people tell me they're going through, have been through or about to go through radiation treatment I have a sincere appreciation and sympathy for what they have to endure. Been there and done that! But the woman, yes, the woman was sitting so patiently reading a book written by Joyce Meyers. I asked her *"Is that a good book you're reading?"*

"Why, yes. It's by Joyce Meyers." Well Margie and I became good friends and we exchanged emails to send words of encouragement and to update one another on our progress. Margie and I emailed one another to encourage each other and others. Here is one of her emails.

Hi Greg,

This is Margie the woman from the cancer place where we talked, and talked about God.

First I want to thank you for your encouragement, as I realized I really needed that. I hope we put some "seeds" in other hearts.

I want you to know, I used our meeting in our church testimony time. I really think people took it to heart. People MUST know to follow the Holy Spirit as He will only lead us to good. Once again, thanks for all you did for me but especially FOR THE LORD!!!!!!!! You will be blessed mightily.

Have a wonderful day and remember: IF YOU WERE THE ONLY PERSON ON EARTH, GOD WOULD HAVE CREATED THIS DAY JUST FOR YOU!! ENJOY IT!!

Margie

Here was another correspondence from Margie.

I have another testimony for you. Remember I told you the Holy Spirit told me God would heal me? I didn't and still don't know his time table, but today I got the results of my MRI for my brain. THERE WAS NOT A PIECE OF IT THERE. IT WAS ALL CLEAR!! Now…is God good or what? I still have my pet scan to go and the doctor is "suspicious" of 2 spots, but I have the Lord's word and I know He does not lie. If I have the cancer back then we'll work through that too. It must be some reason why it came back, and God knew it would and He still told me about the healing. What I think is so grand He knows the beginning to the end and once He says you are healed, as far as He is concerned you are. He knows all the "stuff" you have to go through, so it is nice to have Him "running the show".

I just wanted to tell you and give you testimony of the Lord's word.

To change the subject. I also used the magic mouth wash. It does help, but I only used it when I first started chemo. I did use it again when this infection came on. It is pretty good stuff…just does not last long.

Ok, Greg, hang in there and remember we have someone who's might has never and will never be matched: therefore no one can hurt us and He will be with us every minute of every day and night, and remember Greg, if you get too tired… HE WILL CARRY YOU!!

love
Margie

Boy, you can just tell though when the treatment starts to get you or someone else down. It just wears on you and it beats you down. Once I started the radiation treatment I was doing it five days a week for six weeks and chemotherapy once a week on Wednesdays. I would go to work in the morning, leave around 1:00 PM for my 1:30 PM radiation treatment.

After the second week of radiation, I could tell my body was starting to feel the effects of it all and the chemo was enhancing it even more. So I informed my boss that I would not be returning to work until I finished my treatment because the effects were starting to kick in. So cancer treatment is like a train going up a hill. First, it starts off slow and you kind of creep along with the radiation. Week one and two are okay. However, by the end of week three going into week four…the train starts picking up speed and the pain is like the train going up a huge hill. Then week four the train is over the crest and now it's coming down hill and you're standing in front of it trying to hold the train/pain back. All the while, you are losing weight, you can't eat anything. I remember the last time I tried to eat a bowl of Campbell's Chicken Noodle soup. You know the soup! It's got that tiny little piece of chicken! That little piece of chicken felt like a cinder block in my throat and even the soft noodles felt like ragged rope being wrenched in my throat! It was so painful. So here are a few pictures of the ordeal I did weekly.

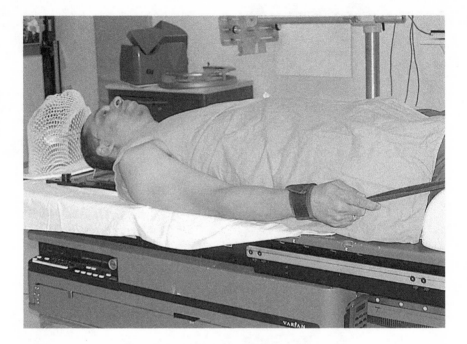

Preparation for radiation treatment. Notice the white mask that they made to pin my head in postion. I was locked down on the table for the duration of the treatment which lasted about a half an hour to forty five mintues.

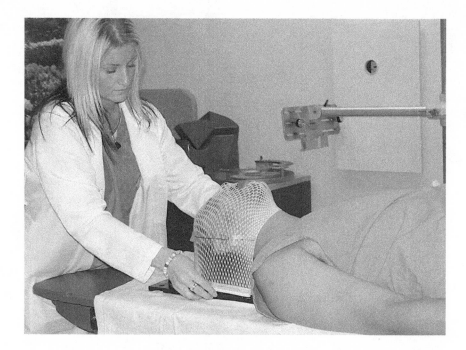

Here the nurse is assisting me getting me ready to start treatment. She's locking my mask in place so my head will not move at all during the treatment as this was precision targeted radiation treatment.

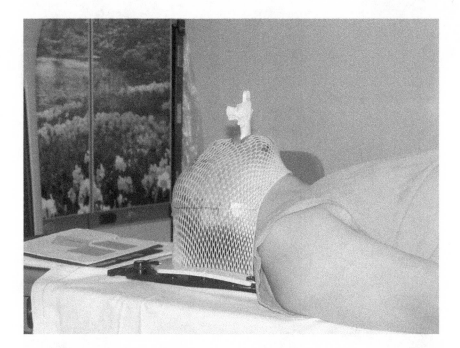

Even my tongue had a piece to keep it from moving during treatment.

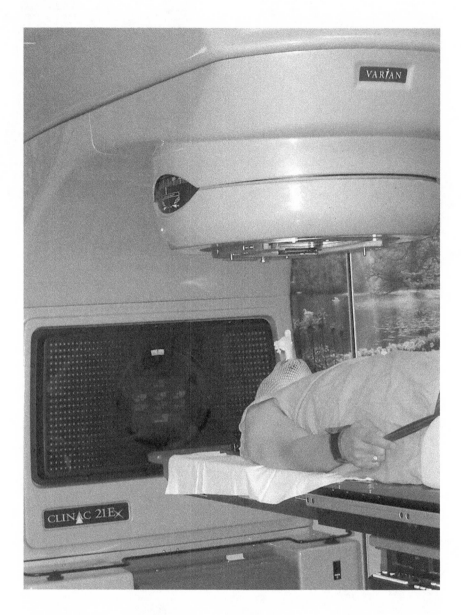

Undergoing the radiation treatment. They targeted six areas in my head and neck for treatment.

This is how I looked when done. As you can see they made sure I didn't move during the process. I had to do this thirty times, five days a week for six weeks.

CHAPTER 29

MY TWENTY-FIRST RADIATION TREATMENT

By my twenty-first radiation treatment my doctor called me into his office and asked me if I knew about the final phase of the treatment, brachytherapy. I informed him that I knew they were doing something different but didn't know all the details. So he sat me down in his office and told me, ***"You need to know what we're going to do…and it's not going to be pretty, but you need to know the details."*** Well by now, I had third-degree burns on my face; I was losing my hair and on a feeding tube now and hearing the details of this procedure was just too much for me to hear. My doctor had described to me, in gross anatomy detail, the brachytherapy treatment they were going to do. This is where they were going to wire my mouth shut, implant eighteen catheters in under my chin, put a trachea tube in my throat and then do radiation seeding for four days while I would reside in the Surgical ICU at Holy Cross Hospital. For those of you who can't picture this…(see below).

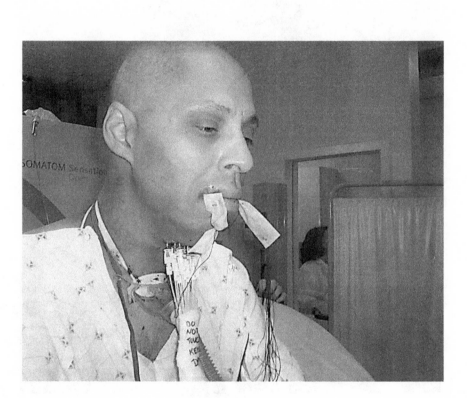

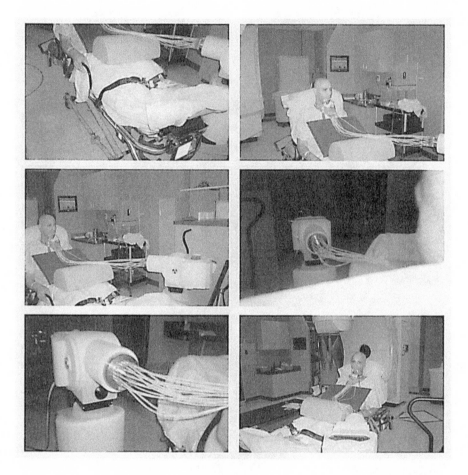

Final Phase of Treatment 2006. Brachytheraphy, Radiation Seeding.

CHAPTER 30

THE MIRACLE! JESUS CAME TO ME!

After hearing the horrific news from my doctor about this treatment all I could do was get in my car and call my wife. She heard how upset I was and asked me if I wanted her to come home, but I told her I would be okay. I just needed to go home and rest. I knew she could hear how distraught and depressed I was from this news. So I went home and I crawled into bed and I said this prayer; *"Lord Jesus, I need you to come to me and tell me something that will help me get through this. I can't take any more and I am ready to quit. I just can't take it, so please come to me and tell me something that will get me through this. I am going to wait here until I hear from you."* I had resolved in my heart that I was not moving or saying another word until Jesus Christ Himself spoke to me that day. Well, let me remind you I was on a lot of pain meds for this treatment, i.e., two Percocet every three hours and two transdermal morphine patches just to manage the pain.

So as I laid there I started to doze off and just before I fell asleep, I heard this voice say to me, *"My son, I am with you. Do not worry. If you permit this and then you testify in My name, I will testify your name to My Father in Heaven."* As I gained consciousness, I sat up in bed and repeated His words, but the part I remembered most was *"testify your name to My Father in Heaven."* All I could think at the time was, *"It doesn't get any higher than that!"* And then the reality of the meds hit me and so I said out loud, *"Lord, did I just hear you correctly? I am not doubting you, but I am on a lot of meds right now and I don't want this to be a figment of my imagination."*

"You said, My son, I am with you. Do not worry. If you permit this and then you testify in My name, I will testify your name to My Father in Heaven." I repeated it so I would not forget His words. And the Lord, Jesus Christ Himself was in the room with me and He said *"I AM with you."* Then the most amazing thing happened to me! I felt Jesus' presence standing right there and I felt as if His hand started at my head and passed through my body and I know He was there because the pain that I had been in for days was now gone! AMEN and PRAISE GOD! When I sensed that He had passed through my head and neck and He got to my chest, tears started rolling down my face and all I could think to say was, *"This is what it's like not to feel pain."* I had been in pain so long that I didn't know what it felt like not to have it. So I laid back down and I felt the most amazing sense of PEACE and JOY I had ever felt! Jesus Christ, our Lord and Savior, came to my room and He touched me and removed my pain.

Okay... This note is for the skeptics. I hear it now... *"Okay, Greg, how do you know it was Jesus who spoke to you?"* The answer is simple. ONLY Jesus used and uses the term *"My Father in Heaven."* But to give you even more validation I have Scriptural proof these were His words and that He said them to me.

So I finished all of my treatment Friday, July 14, 2006. I went to my last treatment in the morning and right into surgery to remove the catheters and trachea tube and the rest of that stuff. However, the effects of the radiation were still in full effect and the recovery time was very slow. I wasn't able to go back to work until the first week in September. I always looked forward to going to church and since I could not go there yet, every Saturday morning I would put on a Bible video and I would have *"church."* Well, this one morning I was watching the Book of Matthew on DVD and it even had the Bible verses in the corner. As I was laying there watching the video it got to Matthew 10 verse 32. *"³²Therefore whoever confesses Me before men, him I will also confess before My Father who is in heaven. ³³ But whoever denies Me before men, him I will also deny before My Father who is in heaven."* I heard the words and thought, wait a minute… I've heard that before! I got up and ran and got my Bible and looked up the verse. Here it is! Here is the absolute proof that I knew with all my heart that Jesus was with me that day! He knew I would find this verse and knew that I would forever hold on to His promise to mention my name to His Father in Heaven. Jesus made a covenant with me that day that was personal for me and to me. I have done my best to keep my end of the covenant too. Every chance I get I try to share the Good News of what Jesus has done for me.

THE LAST DAY OF TREATMENT

I remember that day. The ambulance service came in to pick me up from the Surgical ICU and take me down the street to the radiologists. They wheeled my bed through the hospital and got me outside to the ambulance and strapped me in. They took me inside and I waited as usual for them to take me in the back. When they attached all the catheters to the machine that does the treatment I watched the nurse as she saw me going through the very last treatment. It was bitter-sweet. She was a real comfort to me during the entire ordeal. I looked at her and whispered *"I love you. Thank you."* She whispered back, *"I love you too."* Shortly after, I heard the doctors say, *"WE GOT IT! WE GOT ALL THE CANCER! WE GOT IT!"* They were cheering and very happy that we were done with my treatment, as was I.

A few weeks after I completed treatment, Margie's daughter called to inform me that her mother was back in the hospital and it did not look good for her. I asked her if she wanted me to come pray with her. She was happy to permit my request. She also informed me that her mother was concerned about her father because he was not a believer in Jesus Christ. I felt that this was the Lord calling me to visit my friend, not for her sake, but for her husband's sake. He was saying *"goodbye"* to his dear wife who struggled with cancer and he didn't know where his faith stood.

When I got to the hospital, I went to Margie's room and her husband and daughter were there. I introduced myself and they welcomed me in. Margie was unconscious and still like a lamb sleeping. I asked her daughter what happened and she just told me that she had taken a turn for the worse recently and was back in the hospital. The doctors did not give her long to live. I knew then that whatever I said it could have permanent and eternal impressions on her husband, so I spoke to him: *"You know, I didn't get to know Margie very well, but what I do know is that she was very concerned about your 'spiritual well-being' and that she wanted you to come to know Jesus Christ as your Lord and Savior. She was confident that God would heal her because of the Promise He made to her. So do not worry about her life. She is Saved by the blood of Jesus Christ. The question is, will 'you' be saved right now, in her presence? Will you allow Jesus Christ to be 'your Lord and Savior'?"* With tears rolling down his face, he said *"Yes, I will receive Him."* I prayed over Margie and I prayed with the husband and daughter and told them if they ever needed me, I was just a phone call or email away. It was heartbreaking to see Margie lying there but I know, as do many of you reading these words, that was not the end for Margie. In the day that Jesus Christ returns in all His Glory, **SHE WILL BE RESURRECTED FROM THE DEAD and SHE WILL BE MADE NEW! AMEN AND AMEN!**

CHAPTER 31

SEPTEMBER 2008: ROUTINE PET SCAN

So for inquiring minds, after I went through this type of treatment with radiation and chemotherapy I had to get tested EVERY THREE MONTHS. I had to get full body scans, MRIs and PET scans for the next FIVE YEARS. This is the critical time when you could have reoccurrence of the cancer coming back. So the doctors have to make certain that there are no traces and that's why they do all the testing.

For two years I was fine... However, in September 2008 the routine PET scan showed *"something"* and my doctor called me in to do a routine biopsy. No problem. We've done that before and it proved nothing was there. And sure enough, the results came back negative. Two weeks later though, I was driving back to work from lunch when I got a phone call from my ENT doctor, Dr. Brian, who did the biopsy. *"Hi, Gregory. This is Dr. Brian. I need to see you right away. Your cancer's come back. We made a mistake and read the wrong report from May, not the one you just did. We confirmed with two pathologists and they both confirmed that your cancer has come back. I need to see you tomorrow so we can get you started on your plan of treatment."* When I heard these words my heart just dropped! Here I was thinking everything was okay and now it wasn't. Worst of all, how was I going to tell my wife? She is going to be devastated. So I called her, shared the doctor's news, and told her not to worry and that *"The Lord saw us through this before and He will see us through this again."* Meanwhile, we were planning my fiftieth birthday party and making a list of all the people we intended to invite and now we didn't know if we should continue with the party.

Friday morning, September 12, 2008, Minerva and I were at Dr. Brian's office where he explained to us how sorry he was for the error that they read the wrong report, but more importantly, he wanted to get me over to NIH (National Institutes of Health) first thing Monday morning to start preparing me for possibly the worst radiation and chemotherapy treatment I could imagine... AGAIN.

CHAPTER 32

THE DOCUMENTATION: 2006

The following information are actual scans of the records and documentation taken from my personal medical records book which kept detailed records of all my treatments and the outcomes of all tests taken during that time.

Oral Pathology Services
Maryland Oral Diagnosis and Therapeutics
Tenley Medical Building, Suite 402
50 W. Edmonston Drive, Rockville, MD 20852 • Tel: 301-838-9033 • Fax: 301-838-9148

Patient Name:	Glaude, Gregory	**Tissue Submitted by:** Musgrove ENT Associates
Address:		**Address:** 2415 Musgrove Road
		Suite 201
Gender:	Male	Silver Spring, MD 20901
DOB:	11-01-1958	
SSN:	Not available	

Specimen Source: Base of tongue, left.
Clinical History: 49-year-old male who has undergone chemo- and radiotherapy for T4 squamous cell carcinoma at left base of tongue since May, 2006 and came up for follow-up examination.
Pre-Op Diagnosis: None specified.
Operative Findings: Laryngoscopic biopsy at left base of tongue was performed.
Post-Op Diagnosis: The same as Pre-Op diagnosis.

Pathological Report
(Gross Description, Histologic Examination and Diagnosis)

Surgical Pathology Laboratory   Pathology Accession Number:2008-0674

Gross: One H. & E. stained microslide labeled MD08-10805, Glaude, G., 10-07-2008 and recuts, 10-09-2008, and IHC slides for cytokeratin (cam5.2/AE1/AE3), S-100, CD20 and CD3, a mucicarmine stained slide, 10-17-2008 from GenPath-A Specialized BioReference Laboratory, Clarksburg, MD, were received on 10-07-2008 and 10-17-2008 respectively.

Microscopic: Performed on 10-17-2008.

Diagnosis: Left base of tongue: Recurrent or residual squamous cell carcinoma.

Note: The microscopic foci of carcinoma nest and individual cell(s) appear deeply embedded or infiltrative, which are strongly positive for cytokeratin (cam5.2/AE1/AE3) and negative for others. Clinical correlation is required. The case is consulted by Dr. Gary Ellis at ARUP laboratories, who concurs the diagnosis (see attached consultation report). The case is communicated with Dr. Ian Driscoll on 10-22-2008.

Pathologist:
Di Sun, D.D.S., Ph.D.

Date Collected:	**Date Received:**	**Date Reported:**
October 03, 2008	October 07, 2008	October 17, 2008

124

Diagnosis: Left base of tongue: Recurrent or residual squamous cell carcinoma.

Note: The microscopic foci of carcinoma nest and individual cell(s) appear deeply embedded or infiltrative, which are strongly positive for cytokeratin (cam5.2/AE1/AE3) and negative for others. Clinical correlation is required. The case is consulted by Dr. Gary Ellis at ARUP laboratories, who concurs the diagnosis (see attached consultation report). The case is communicated with Dr. Ian Driscoll on 10-22-2008.

Pathologist:
Dr. Sun, D.D.S., Ph.D.

This was the biopsy done in October of 2008.

Psychosocial History: He says that he was a smoker and smoke almost a pack of cigarettes per day for 30 years, and he quite in 2000. He previously consumed approximately two alcohol beverages per day, but has not had any alcohol since the diagnosis of the squamous cell cancer.

Physical Examination:

General: Patient is well-appearing.

ENT Examination: Unremarkable. Extraocular movements are intact. Oropharynx clear without any exudate or erythema.

Neck: Small 7 cm mobile right submandibular node is nontender and palpable. Otherwise, no significant findings on the neck is seen.

Cardiac: Regular rate and rhythm. No murmurs appreciated.

Pulmonary: Clear to auscultation bilaterally.

Abdomen: Soft, nontender, nondistended. Positive bowel sounds.

Extremities: No clubbing or edema noted.

Neurologically: His cranial nerves are grossly intact. Motor is 5/5 in both upper and lower extremities, and sensation is intact.

CLINICAL DIAGNOSIS:

This is a 49-year-old patient with history of T4 N0 M0 squamous cell cancer, which is now T4 N0 M0 stage IVA squamous cell cancer of the left base of the tongue, here status post definitive chemoradiation, now presenting with recurrence and wants further evaluation regarding our bortezomib with radiation treatment.

TESTS/PROCEDURES AND DATES PERFORMED:

1. On September 18, 2008, an MRI (magnetic resonance imaging) of the tongue and oropharynx were performed.

2. September 11, 2008, a PET (positron emission tomography) scan was performed.

Date of Visit: 10/27/2008   FIRST REGISTRATION OUTPATIENT REPORT

Patient Identification
Glaude, Gregory Austin   44-64-66-7

-3-

Outpatient Record
NIH-532-8 (7-99)
P.A. 09-25-0099
File in Section 1: Summaries, Operations,
                    History & Physical Exam

MEDICAL RECORD

Date of Visit: 10/27/2008

DICTATOR IDENTIFICATION:

Name:	Nabila Chowdhury, M.D.
Office Address:	Bldg. 10 Rm. 12N226
Office Telephone:	301-496-4916

HISTORY AND PHYSICAL EXAMINATION AND SIGNIFICANT FINDINGS:

Purpose of Encounter: Patient is a 49-year-old male with history of CT4 N0 M0 stage IVA squamous cell cancer at the left base of the tongue, status post definitive chemoradiation, presenting with radiographic and pathologic evidence of disease, returns for evaluation and re-irradiation.

History of Present Illness: Patient initially presented in March with progressive peritonsillar discomfort and jaw pain radiating to the left side of the head. The patient was seen by primary care provider and referred to Otorhinolaryngology. No abnormalities were seen on endoscopic examination at that time, and patient was referred for an MRI of the neck performed on April 6, 2006, which revealed a prominent left tonsillar pillar with soft tissue edema with pillar enhancement and asymmetry, as well as evidence of deep extrinsic muscles of the tongue involvement. Patient underwent an esophagram on April 24, 2006, which revealed soft tissue mass near the base of the tongue. Then he underwent base of the tongue biopsy on April 26, 2008, which revealed poorly differentiated squamous cell carcinoma at the base of the tongue, and he was designated to have T4 disease. On a metastatic workup, including a PET scan that was obtained on May 1, 2006, which revealed a 4.3 cm large irregular left tongue base mass, with an SUV of 18.8, and a mass that extended to the intrinsic tongue muscles, consistent with the patient's known diagnosis of squamous cell cancer. The patient was treated with definitive chemoradiation concurrently, and he received IMRT using 6 mV photons and 7 treatment plan to the tongue and neck with involved disease, removing 60 grays in 30 fractions. In the

Date of Visit: 10/27/2008   FIRST REGISTRATION OUTPATIENT REPORT

Mr. Glaude is a 49-year-old male with history of cT4 N0 M0 left base of tongue squamous cell carcinoma, status-post definitive chemoradiation, presenting with pathology proven disease recurrence at the base of tongue for evaluation of potential re-irradiation.

PLAN:

At this time, the patient is pending his formal consultation with the Otorhinolaryngology Branch. However, as per Head and Neck Tumor Board discussion, he is likely not a surgical candidate at this time. Additionally, the patient strongly wishes to avoid surgery if at all possible and wishes to consider re-irradiation as part of his treatment for his disease recurrence. Planned definitive re-irradiation would be administered with concurrent chemotherapy, and the patient will be in contact with medical oncology for evaluation. The patient also has not been seen by a dentist since 2006, and we will arrange for the patient to be seen by a dentist at the National Institutes of Health on October 29, 2008. Additionally, as the patient had a history of a G-tube placement in May 2006 during his prior course of radiation therapy, we will likely encourage the patient to have a prophylactic G-tube placement. Therefore, we will arrange for the patient to be seen by Surgery for G-tube placement. We will also obtain a swallowing study to evaluate his current functioning and repeat a PET scan to further evaluate the sublingual space abnormality seen on outside hospital PET scan from September 11, 2008, as well as to evaluate for any additional metastatic disease. The risks and benefits of radiation therapy were discussed in detail with the patient. It was stressed that re-irradiation to this region is associated with significantly increased risk of toxicity when compared with his definitive irradiation that the patient underwent in May and June 2006. So as to minimize any potential dose to the spinal cord, we will consider placing fiducial markers in the base of tongue or in a bite block or perform another means of daily target localization for radiation therapy. These markers will be placed prior to his PET scan so that images can be registered and fused to aid in treatment planning. Should the patient wish to proceed with definitive re-irradiation and wish to receive treatment at the National Institutes of Health, we will perform a CT simulation in the supine position with a mask for immobilization. In the interim, we will have the patient's pathology from October 3, 2008, formally reviewed by the Pathology Branch at the National Institutes of Health. We will be in touch with the patient to coordinate his additional studies and for further treatment recommendations.

This patient was seen and examined with Dr. Nicole Simone, who agrees with the above.

Date of Visit: 10/27/2008

Patient Identification
Glaude, Gregory Austin   44-64-66-7

-5-

Radiation Oncology
History and Physical Examination
NIH-2435-4 (7-97)
P.A. 09-25-0099
File In Section 3, Radiation Therapy
DO NOT FILE IN MEDICAL RECORD

When we arrived at NIH, there was a barrage of things we had to do to register as a patient and get in their system for repeat visits. Then we met Dr. Brian in his office and he explained that before they could start any treatment I would basically have to be approved by several of the doctors on staff there to see if I could even *"survive"* the treatment since they do not do *"Head and Neck Radiation Treatment"* more than once. This was a very dangerous procedure to attempt this a second time because of all the physical damage done to me the first time. I still have a lot of scarring to this day because of the dramatic form of radiation therapy and brachytherapy I received before. My life was indeed, in grave danger. Chances of survival diminished greatly in the face of having to do my previous treatment all over again. However, all the way through this I kept telling my wife and myself, *"The Lord saw us through this before and He will see us through this again."* And I truly believed that. I would allow nothing or no one tell me any different, despite the odds of survival.

CHAPTER 33

PREPPING FOR TREATMENT

So from September 2008 until the end of October 2008 we saw every doctor, dentist and nurse imaginable that had to approve me to go through the radiation, chemotherapy and possible surgical implants that I had endured back in 2006. And while this was very daunting, to say the least, I remember the patients that I met along the way. I kept them in my prayers daily and made a note of them in my journal. Everyone there was either sick themselves or with someone who was gravely sick and needed prayer intervention. I knew that Power of Prayer and how God had healed me before, even though I had to endure a very grueling treatment. I knew God was always with me and He told me so. So during this two-month long period of discovery, as I waited to visit with my doctors I would introduce myself to other patients and ask them why they were there and what they were being treated for. Then, after hearing their stories, I would tell them about Jesus Christ and how He spoke to me during my previous treatment and how He touched me and relieved my pain. Then I would ask them if they wanted me to pray with them for their healing. Not one person ever said, *"No, thank you."*

Every patient I met with always said, ***"Yes. I would like that."*** There is something about *"crisis"* that people relate to. Crisis helps put away *"foolish barriers"* that hold us back from being ***"Loving. Kind. Generous. Forgiving. And Loving Our Neighbors As Ourselves."*** Crisis brings about an awareness of other people's needs, even over our own need. Look at what happened September 11, 2001. Our country was in a *"crisis"* and everyone came to serve others, some to the point of losing their lives!

TWO BROTHERS FROM NEW JERSEY

I remember these two guys from New Jersey who were sitting next to me and one of them was waiting to give blood. I asked one of them why there were at NIH and one of them said to me, ***"My brother is here because he has no white cell blood count. We don't know what's wrong. So we're here to find out what we can do."*** I shared with them my testimony of how God healed me of cancer before and asked them if they wanted me to pray with them. *"Absolutely!"* they said. You know, people who are sick or who have a loved one and in need of healing are the ones who come to Jesus Christ the most. They have a need that goes beyond their abilities and they recognize their insufficiency. You may not convince a healthy person they're in need of Jesus Christ, our Lord and Savior because they have no need of healing, whether physical, spiritual or both. But a person who is sick, believe me, you don't have to convince them of their need! They know they need and moreover, they have a *"desire"* to be healed and Jesus, who bore our sins, **Isaiah 53:5**: But He *was* wounded for our transgressions, *He was* bruised for our iniquities. The chastisement for our peace *was* upon Him, And **by His stripes we are healed**. After my prayer with the two brothers, I never saw them again. However, I know my prayer with them lifted them up and gave them the courage to continue their fight and know that God was on their side.

A WOMAN PREPPING
FOR A PROCEDURE

I remember another time when I was preparing for a procedure and in a room with several other people getting prepped for the same. This one woman looked pretty terrified and worried and I couldn't help but speak with her to try and comfort her. When I told her about my life and the healing I had received before it was like someone had breathed life into her! She was so happy that I shared my testimony with her. As they were wheeling her in on the gurney, she looked back at me and smiled and told me she would never forget me and that she believed that the Lord was going to heal her. Again, I never saw her after that, but I have to trust that God was with her and we'll find out one day when Jesus comes.

The fact is, Jesus Christ, our Lord and Great Physician, is so willing to heal us of our infirmities and sickness because we were never designed or meant to be sick, ever! However, more importantly, this same Jesus Christ also *"Died for our sins!"* that we would never have to die. It is so important for us not to miss this. The *"cleansing of the leper"* was not just to remove the *"leprosy,"* which by the way was an *"incurable"* disease, but to also cleanse him *"spiritually"* and make him whole again. Here are a few Scriptures that support this.

Hebrews 11: By Faith We Understand "FAITH"

[1]Now faith is the substance of things hoped for, the evidence of things not seen.

[6]But without faith *it is* impossible to please *Him*, for he who comes to God must believe that He is, and *that* He is a rewarder of those who diligently seek Him. (**Hebrews 11:1 and 6**)

Matthew 9: A Woman Healed

[20] And suddenly, a woman who had a flow of blood for twelve years came from behind and touched the hem of His garment. [21] For she said to herself, *"If only I may touch His garment, I shall be made well."* [22] But Jesus turned around, and when He saw her He said, "Be of good cheer, daughter; *your faith has made you well."* And the woman was made well from that hour.

Matthew 9: Two Blind Men Healed

[32] As they went out, behold, they brought to Him a man, mute and demon-possessed. [33] And when the demon was cast out, the mute spoke. And the multitudes marveled, saying, *"It was never seen like this in Israel!"* [34] But the Pharisees said, *"He casts out demons by the ruler of the demons.*

[29] Then He touched their eyes, saying, *"According to your faith let it be to you."* [30] And their eyes were opened. And Jesus sternly warned them, saying, *"See that no one knows it."* [31] But when they had departed, they spread the news about Him in all that country."

Matthew 9: A Mute Man Speaks

[27] When Jesus departed from there, two blind men followed Him, crying out and saying, *"Son of David, have mercy on us!"* [28] And when He had come into the house, the blind men came to Him. And Jesus said to them, *"Do you believe that I am able to do this?"* They said to Him, *"Yes, Lord."*

There are so many other Scriptures to share about the compassion of our God through Christ Jesus and His *"willingness to heal us."* The question we have to ask ourselves is: *"Are we willing to be healed and are we willing to believe by faith that Jesus Christ is not only "able" but "willing to heal" as well."*

It is our absolute faith and belief in Jesus Christ that heals us and ultimately, saves us.

As we take our walk with God, there are so many roadways and highways upon the earth that we may travel. However, it is the *"narrow road of faith"* that leads us to the Healing Grace of God in Christ Jesus that permits us to receive His blessings of healing and of restoration.

Now I know some of you are saying and even asking the question: *"I've prayed and I've believed and nothing happened. I've prayed over loved ones, even anointed them and they still passed on! So I don't believe this works."* And there is the problem. We do not understand the *"faith"* portion to understand how God works in all this. He is not a candy machine that if we insert money, we get out what we want. We first must *"align ourselves with God's will."* Period. And in doing so, our thoughts and our desires will align with the Father's. Jesus did not do His own will, He did what the Father instructed Him to do, ALWAYS! Jesus was perfectly aligned with the Father's will, even unto death, even death on the Cross. Now I am going to share something that you may not agree with but here it is. As we pray for loved ones who are sick, especially those who are *"terminally ill"* we often pray for healing, to which God always answers one way or another. Sometimes the answer is healing in this life, and sometimes not. What we need to know and understand (here it comes) is that, *"Death can also bring healing."* Now I know that sounds strange. However, understand this from an *"eternal"* point of view. No one will take sickness with them on the other side of eternity. AMEN! And that's a good thing! If your mother or father died of cancer, that murderous disease will not end up following them on the other side of eternity. **ALL DISEASE SICKNESS, and SUFFERING will come to an end.** So in this life, when we pray for loved ones or ourselves to be healed, God always answers that prayer. It just may not be the way we would like or hope. Just remember, God is also, MERCIFUL! How often have people who have loved ones who have been injured in accidents or terminally ill prayed that they would be spared sickness, pain and suffering, asked God to *"heal"* them? And God does… in His own way. Death is a healer to many lives that have suffered enormous pain and agony. We have all heard it or said it ourselves, *"They're in a better place now. They aren't suffering anymore."* You are absolutely correct. They are not suffering anymore. The fact is, often times we are the ones suffering at the loss of someone very dear to us and we do not want to let go.

CHAPTER 34

11/01/2008: THE FIFTIETH BIRTHDAY PARTY

During these days of going back and forth to NIH my wife and I had been discussing what we were going to do for my birthday celebration, in light of preparing for a horrific ordeal of cancer treatment, again. We had already devised a wonderful celebration and sent out the invitations but she was having second thoughts about having it. So my wife asked me again if I still wanted to have the party, to which I replied, *"Absolutely! If I am going to go through cancer treatment again I want to go in pumped up and rejoicing that we had a good time!"* So we did! We invited about fifty of our closest friends to a party like none before! We asked everyone to dress up as their favorite singer or musician and they had to bring a song on disc to *"lip-sync"* their song and they would be judged on their performance! It was amazing and we had a great time! We had the driveway lit up with spotlights, a red carpet leading up the driveway into the house and even the red velvet ropes like you see in Hollywood! And to make my entrance while everyone was waiting on the red carpet outside, I pulled up in a tricked-out Dodge Magnum that one of my clients owned! It had a two-toned paint job, custom twenty-two-inch rims, and a huge sound system in the back, which made for an awesome entrance to the party! The neighbors were looking out the windows to see what the heck was going on! I'll tell you, *"It was Party Time!"* We had everyone from Jimi Hendrix, to Prince, to Madonna, to Michael and Janet

Jackson, Celia Cruz, and many more! Everyone was amazing and no one knew a thing about my cancer returning. We did not want to spoil the mood and have people feeling sad and sorry. So we kept silent about the reoccurrence of my cancer and made it the BEST fiftieth birthday celebration EVER! It was a most memorable occasion and everyone truly enjoyed themselves!

NOVEMBER 2, 2008
THE ANOINTING AND THE
WRONG PRAYER

So the next day was Sunday and while I still had the sports car I borrowed from a client, we decided to visit some friends, Gary and Linda, and, let their son see the car. Now Gary and Linda were both at my party the night before. When we got to their home, we sat down as usual just to talk and Linda, said these words: *"You all are going through something and you haven't told us."* So I looked at my wife and said, *"Did you tell them?"*

"No, I didn't." And my wife replied to Linda saying, *"Well… Greg's cancer has returned."* Well, their kids were there, and one started crying.

Well, I have to interject a note here: *You can have NO BETTER FRIEND, than one who will PRAY FOR YOU. PERIOD!*

So when my wife said that, Gary immediately replied, *"Well, I'm going to get the oil and we're going to anoint you and pray over you for your healing."* HERE IS THE KEY! If you are a Believer in the Word of God and call yourself a Christian then when you hear that someone is sick, this should be your response… EVERY TIME!

MEETING SPECIFIC NEEDS

[13] Is anyone among you suffering? Let him pray. Is anyone cheerful? Let him sing psalms. [14] Is anyone among you sick? Let him call for the elders of the church, and let them pray over him, **anointing him with oil in the name of the Lord.** [15] And the prayer of faith will save the sick, and the Lord will raise him up. And if he has committed sins, he will be forgiven. [16] **Confess *your* trespasses to one another, and pray for one another, that you may be healed.** The effective, fervent prayer of a righteous man avails much. **(James 5:13–16, NKJV)**

Boy, oh boy, I let that prayer they prayed over me sink in. All day long I kept that prayer on my heart, so much so, as I was driving to work the next morning and hearing the words of **Matthew 9:20–22 (NKJV),** [20] And suddenly, a woman who had a flow of blood for twelve years came from behind and touched the hem of His garment. [21] For she said to herself, *"If only I may touch His garment, I shall be made well."* [22] But Jesus turned around, and when He saw her He said, *"Be of good cheer, daughter; your faith has made you well."* And the woman was made well from that hour.

After reflecting on the Words of Matthew, I said to the Lord Jesus, *"Lord! I have been praying the WRONG PRAYER! I don't want you to "see me through" this cancer, I want you to heal me! The woman who had flow of blood for twelve years said to herself, "If I may touch His garment, I would be made well." And she was! She was healed because of her faith! Lord, I am grabbing hold of your garment and I am not letting go until you heal me!"* And from that moment on I believed that Jesus Christ, our Great Physician, healed me of my infirmities and never looked back. From that moment on, I believed that the Power of Prayer in Jesus was my way to my healing and not the cancer treatment with radiation and chemotherapy.

ONE CAVEAT HERE
ABOUT TREATMENT

Please know my dear friends, **I AM NOT SAYING DO NOT DO RADIATION OR CHEMO TREATMENT** in lieu of prayers! Please do not misquote me or believe that I am saying don't do treatment, *"If you need treatment."*

Here is what I am saying. I got *"PROOF!"* So this was Monday and now later that week on Thursday, November 6, 2008 my doctor had scheduled me for a biopsy at NIH to see where the cancer was in order to update my diagnosis. Well, Wednesday evening, my wife and another friend and I got on our knees to pray about the upcoming procedure the next morning. During the prayer, I remember we kept claiming God's Healing Power and we *"believed by faith that God had healed me."* When we were done I got up from the floor I just started proclaiming that I had been healed! I kept proclaiming that I knew God had healed me. Now mind you, I did NOT feel any special *"overtaking of the Holy Spirit"* or *"Holy Spirit moment knocking me to the floor."* There was no *"feeling"* at all. There was indeed though the *"peace and comfort"* knowing that I had been healed and that was enough. And boy was it is enough. God does not always *"Knock us over!"* to heal us. In fact, I don't know of any Scripture that says when Jesus healed someone, or even the Disciples, that upon doing so they were knocked over by the Holy Spirit.

CHAPTER 35

THURSDAY: NOVEMBER 6, 2008

The next morning it was the two-year anniversary of my mother's passing and Minerva and I were up very early, around 5:30 AM as we had to be at NIH at 7:30 AM for the biopsy procedure. We arrived on time and walking through the dark parking garage I remember looking at my wife and we both were still on that spiritual high knowing that God had healed me. We were completely convinced. No one was going to tell us any differently.

When we arrived at NIH and were in preparation for surgery, the nurses were talking with us, and when we told them that *"We've prayed about this and God has healed me!"* The nurses were all in agreement with us and said, *"We are Believers too! You tell those doctors what God has done for you!"* Well that just fueled my fire even more!

When Dr. Brian (my ENT) and Dr. Liesl (new doctor on board) came to my bedside right before surgery they asked, *"How are you doing this morning Mr. Glaude?"*

"Excellent!"

"Excellent? No one says 'excellent' before going into surgery. What's going on?" I told them. *"Don't be surprised."*

"Surprised?"

"Yes. My wife and I prayed about this and God has healed me!" Well, the two doctors were just taken by surprise! They didn't know what to think or say. Stunned into quiet and not knowing how to reply, they looked at my wife and asked, *"What's going on?"* And my wife confirmed what I said and repeated it, *"Yes, he's been healed by God and that's it!"* Well, all the doctors could do was agree with us. They never encountered anyone who was, just two months prior, diagnosed with cancer and confirmed by two separate pathologists that the cancer was indeed there, and now the patient is claiming to be healed by God. *"Okay, Mr. Glaude. Well, I'm glad you're thinking positive."* I said, *"No, I'm not thinking positive. I'm trying to tell you so you're prepared. I've been healed!"* Well, both doctors were now puzzled even more and thought maybe we should get him in surgery so we can answer this once and for all. So let me share with you what this biopsy involves. It starts with me getting an IV (intravenous drip) put in and then waiting to go into surgery. Once there, they sedate you and the procedure lasts about a half an hour. It's usually pretty quick if they know where the cancer is, and they did. During the procedure, they take little hollow needles and they poke the area and take a sample of the tissue. And the deeper the cancer is under the tissue, the deeper they have to go to get the sample. In my case, the cancer was under my tongue, so they had to go really deep into the tissue to get the sample.

Now, as I mentioned, the procedure normally takes about a half an hour. On this day they took over two hours. Not to mention, with all the medical staff needed for the procedure, they also had a pathologist in the operating room with them to determine if the sample taken was indeed cancerous. By this time my wife was getting nervous and thinking something must have gone wrong. When Dr. Brian came out to my wife, she said she noticed his hands were *"visibly shaking"* and that he was very nervous and it scared her. When he came to her he said, *"Greg is all right…but we are just puzzled. We don't know what happened."* And my wife paused and said, *"What do you mean?"*

"Well, we don't know what happened but we can't find the cancer." My wife burst into laughter! And then she reminded him, *"Don't you remember what he told you?"*

He said, *"Don't be surprised!"* The doctor was still just confused about what happened. So my wife said to him, *"I want to be there when you tell him. I want to see his face."*

So now, I am in the recovery room just waking up and Dr. Brian came to me and asked how I felt. *"A little sore. You must have done a lot of tests."* Well when I looked at him I noticed his face and his expression did not look like he had good news. So I asked him, *"What's wrong, Doc?"*

"Well, we're a little puzzled."

"What do you mean?"

"Well, we've tested every area of the base of your tongue and we can't find any cancer."

"Baahahhahahah! Doc! I told you "Don't be surprised!" and look! I don't have cancer!"

Well, he was not so convinced of the healing 100%. In fact his reply was, *"Well, we don't want to get too excited here. We're going to have to run so more tests. We'll get them back by Monday."*

"You do your tests. All you're going to do is confirm that I don't have cancer!" WOWWW! What a VICTORY for Christ Jesus! People always here about *"miraculous healings"* but they never seemed to happen to me…until now!

So the next day on Friday morning, NIH had already had me scheduled for a pre-screening X-ray of my throat area as part of one of the tests. As soon as the attending nurse turned on the machine she evidently could see the image of my throat and I heard her say, *"Ohhh my!"*

"What's wrong?" I said.

"You just had a biopsy, didn't you?"

"Yes, ma'am. Just yesterday."

"I could tell because it looks like over one hundred samples were taken and I can see them!" What I realized is that while this procedure normally takes a half an hour, this one took over two hours because they were looking for something that was not there anymore. They were convinced that I had cancer and were determined to find it. However, my faith told them it wasn't so it didn't matter how many samples they took... God healed me.

GOOD NEWS TRAVELS FAST

Well, Monday comes around and I still had to take some tests for preparation for cancer treatment, even though they found no evidence of cancer a few days before. So I went upstairs to Dr. Brian's office on the fifth floor at NIH and his assistant, Dr. Liesl, came to me and informed me that the test results would be in shortly. When she was leaving to get the results I told her before she left, *"The results are going to prove that God has healed me."*

"Well, let's wait and see," she said. Well, I want you to know that the devil will try to get in your head and try to cause you to disbelieve *"even when you have the evidence."* The devil was trying to cause me to doubt but I would not give in. So to distract my ears from hearing his lies, I started singing...yes, out loud! I started praising God for healing me! I started praising God for His Love and Mercy for me! And just a minute later Dr. Liesl walked in the room, *"Well, I guess God has healed you because you don't have can-*

cer!" I was overjoyed! TRULY OVERJOYED! Here it was God had truly answered my prayers and the prayers of others on my behalf and I could not wait to tell everyone!

So I called my wife, Minerva, and told her! And she called Gary and Linda and the news was spreading among the family and friends like wildfire! Well Dr. Brian's office was on the fifth floor and I had to report to oncology which was on lower level, B-2, seven floors down. By the time I got there only five minutes later, the news had gotten down stairs and the receptionist and others there knew about my *"miraculous healing"* and they all acknowledged my special moment. They were all so joyful. Even the head of the department told me how wonderful it was that I was healed because had I gone through treatment I may not have survived. This was just amazing!

When I got home that evening and we were standing around in the kitchen just sharing this good news, my wife's niece, Michelle, called me and said, ***"Hey! I heard about your healing today! That's so cool!"*** I thanked her for the call. I could tell she was indeed happy for me.

CHAPTER 36

THE DOCUMENTATION: 2008

The following information are actual scans of the records and documentation taken from my personal medical records book, which kept detailed records of all my treatments and the outcomes of all tests taken during that time.

Date Performed: 11/06/2008

DICTATOR IDENTIFICATION:

Name:	Brian P Driscoll, M.D.	
Office Address:	Bldg. 10	Rm. 4-2732
Office Telephone:	301-402-4216	

Preoperative Diagnosis: Left base of tongue recurrent squamous cell carcinoma.

Primary Surgeon: Brian P Driscoll, M.D.

First Assistant Surgeon: Liesl K Nottingham, M.D.

Other Assistant Surgeon(s): None.

Operative Diagnosis: Pending.

Title of Operation: Multiple core needle biopsies of the base of tongue.

Specimens of Tissue Sent for
Examination and Destination:
1. Left base of tongue for frozen section times two; nondiagnostic.
2. Left base of tongue.
3. Left anterior base of tongue.
4. Midline base of tongue.
5. Left lateral base of tongue.
6. Right base of tongue.
Specimens 2 through 6 are sent for permanent section.

Estimated Blood Loss (EBL): 20 cubic centimeters.

Complications: None observed.

DESCRIPTION OF OPERATION AND FINDINGS:

Operative Procedure: The patient was taken to the Operating Room where general anesthesia was induced and the patient was intubated. The tablet was then turned 90 degrees. A Jennings mouth gag was placed in the mouth to hold open the mouth. The tongue was then grasped in the midline with a perforating towel clamp. Using a curved tongue

Date of Visit: 11/06/2008   OUTPATIENT OPERATION

blade from the tonsil retractor, the anterior portion of the tongue was retractor and exposed nicely the base of tongue. A biopsy of the left base of tongue was done with an 18-gauge and then a 16-gauge core needle biopsy. These were both sent for permanent section. We looked at the specimens with the pathologist and these were nondiagnostic for squamous cell carcinoma. There was some atypical cells, but they could not make a diagnosis of squamous cell carcinoma. It became apparent in talking to the pathologist that permanent sections are going to be done. Thus, five additional permanent sections were done with a 16-gauge core needle biopsy, and these were from the left base of tongue, the left anterior base of tongue, the midline base of tongue, the left lateral base of tongue, and the right base of tongue. These were all marked at the mucosal edge with methylene blue. The specimens were then sent off for permanent section. At the time of dictation, the patient is currently undergoing the extubation procedure. Prior to this, a small wound in the midline floor of mouth, where the floor of mouth meets the tongue, was closed with 3-0 chromic sutures. Ray-Tecs had been placed in the mouth for 5-10 minutes to stop any bleeding. The mouth was irrigated and there was no bleeding noted at the time of extubation. The patient will followup. It also should be noted that 10 milligrams of Decadron was given in the case to help with any swelling.

CC: Carter Van Waes, M.D.

END OF REPORT

Dictated by:
Brian P Driscoll, M.D. 11/06/2008 10:24 A
Institute/Branch: DC/HN
Transcribed on:
11/06/2008 10:48 A

Signed by:
David A Bianchi, M.D. 11/26/2008 16:27

Date of Visit: 11/06/2008   OUTPATIENT OPERATION

Patient Identification

Glaude, Gregory Austin   44-64-66-7

Outpatient Record
NIH-532-8 (7-99)
P.A. 09-25-0099
File in Section 1: Summaries, Operations,
History & Physical Exam

-2-

So in other words... *"I DON'T HAVE CANCER!"*

"WHO WILL WITNESS TO THEM?"

So two months after being told that I had cancer and it was confirmed by two pathologists and then being tested and prepped for treatment, an amazing thing took place. *"I was healed."* No matter what anyone says about me or about God, I know He and He alone healed me and no one can take that away. I had cancer. Now I don't and without one dose of radiation or chemotherapy. Not one pill was given or a shot taken to remove it. It was my faith in God and what the Bible says about God and His Everlasting Mercy upon us.

So now what? I was healed and yet, NIH still had me coming back and forth for more tests. It seems as if something now had manifested in my chest and throat...something else. Well of course it did. The devil was not happy about my healing and wanted to cause yet another *"symptom."* Here's the thing about *"symptoms."* The devil uses symptoms to cause us to doubt God and His Healing Powers over the sickness. Cast out the symptoms and let your faith take hold. One morning I am driving to NIH and I was praying and asked God, *"Lord, I know you have healed me of cancer. Everyone knows it. So why do I have to keep going back to this place?"* And I want to tell you, the Lord God, Jesus Christ spoke right back at me and said, *"If I don't send you, who will witness to them?"* I submitted to the Lord's calling right then and agreed with Him. How could I not? The Lord had given me the privilege to speak to those who needed encouragement, who needed prayer and He chose me. *"I'll do it."* So for several more months I met people and prayed with them as often as I could. I never met a person I couldn't pray with. I never met a person who said no.

PRAYER MINISTRY: *"WOULD YOU PRAY FOR ME?*

They say, *"Good news travels fast!"* people started hearing about my miraculous healing and wanted to know if I would come and pray with them. I always have made room in my day to go and pray for people. It didn't matter if they were home or in the hospital. I would make the time to go and visit. After all, how can you say *"no"* to someone requesting you to come and pray with them? Well some dear friends, Hank and Lynne, were experiencing some difficult times themselves. Hank, or Dr. Hank, is actually our dentist and we have known him for years, whom, you read about him when I was trying to discover what the pain was in my throat that turned out to be cancer.

One day after getting a routine teeth cleaning and checkup, Hank mentioned to me about his wife's medical procedures and how expensive they were and how concerned he was because of the type of treatment she was having. He wasn't concerned with the money at all. He was concerned that the love of his life had to endure this medical treatment for jaw reconstruction on her face as she had some type of bone cancer and required bone reconstruction and more. One Sunday afternoon my wife and I dropped off some food for them and the family so they wouldn't have to worry about cooking during her time of recovery, which required her to sit in a hyperbaric chamber for cancer survivors and wound care. As we were leaving, I happened to mention to Lynne, *"Hey, Lynne, if you would like us to pray for you we can come and anoint you for your healing and pray for you."* Well, she said she would think about it, and sure enough, the next morning, I got an email bright and early requesting the healing. So with that, I contacted our friends, Gary and Linda, who anointed me for my healing back in 2008. You might be asking yourself, *"Why would he call Gary and Linda to go with him to pray when Lynne asked me to pray over her?"* That's a great question and here is, what I hope to be, a great answer.

Sometimes it's not meant for us, *"me"* to do the anointing but give this gift and share this Powerful Expression of God's Love with someone else. However, there is another reason. Hank knew me as a *"friend and patient"* and has never seen me operate as a *"Minister of the Gospel of Jesus Christ"* and I did not want to ruin the opportunity to minister and witness to the entire family by *"stepping in the way."* So I asked Gary and Linda if they would, not only join us, but perform the anointing as well. Hank and Lynne did not know Gary and Linda well at the time so I thought it more appropriate for Gary to do this special offering anointing so that there would be no prejudice against them.

And as a result, during our prayer time with the six of us, Hank's heart was moved to tears. It touched us all.

The very next time that Lynne went to her doctor she told us that he said this about her condition and recovery, *"Your healing is miraculous!"* and she said *"It is indeed!"* I have seen it over and over where people who, not only believe in the Lord Jesus Christ, but also *"Call upon His name"* receive the healing they ask for and more. How is that so you ask? Well think of it this way. It is one thing to receive the Healing of God, especially under the pressure of a serious disease or health issue, but it is altogether even greater when you get to *"witness to others about what God has done for you!"* in that healing. We have now become *"God's Messengers and His Ministers."* The Bible calls us *"Ambassadors for Christ." "Now then, we are ambassadors for Christ, as though God were pleading through us: we implore you on Christ's behalf, be reconciled to God"* (2 Corinthians 5:20). What an awesome responsibility!

CHAPTER 37

PRISON MINISTRIES: NBCI NORTH BRANCH CORRECTIONAL INSTITUTION

Several years passed by and a dear friend, Gwen, who used to attend our church, had asked me if I would come and teach the Bible study one Sabbath. It was her husband Michael, in fact, who first got me teaching Bible studies at church years before. It was after church one day that she asked me and I inquired as to what the pastor was doing that day. She mentioned that he was going to the prison... *"Prison!? I want to go to the prison. How can I go with them?"* So I sat down with the pastor that afternoon and shared with him my testimony and he agreed with me that I should go to the prison and share this testimony with the men, with this caveat... *"You will preach to the men when we go. You will give the sermon."* I was delighted! I went home and started working on my sermon notes, which turned out more like a dissertation than a sermon, but I was writing away pouring out my heart and adding Scriptures into my notes. Finally, a few weeks later on a Friday afternoon, pastor called me and said, *"We're going to the prison tomorrow. You will be ready to go, yes?"*

Well, of course I would be ready. Pastor JJ Moses was not much on giving advance notice. However, that was just his way. He lived by a different set of rules than we do. If he knew something in his mind that was what mattered. The fact that he told me at all was important enough.

The next day, Sabbath afternoon, I met the pastor at his house and he and I drove two hours in his nice Jaguar sedan all the way out to Cumberland, MD to the maximum security prison there, NBCI (North Branch Correctional Institution). As we approached the prison we got over this slight hill and then, BAMMM! There was the prison! It was full of barb-wire and extended for what seemed like miles! It took my breath away to see this massive expanse of prison, especially knowing that all sorts of men were locked up here and there was no way they would escape such a place. I took a deep breath as we rounded the corner of the prison. We drove about another half mile and then pulled into the entrance and parked. As we entered the building there were these massive metal doors that seemed like only Goliath could open. As we approached the front desk there were about three guards at the front desk and they did not seem very friendly. Pastor asked if we could go in and the one lady who resembled the old lady on the bicycle in the beginning of the Wizard of Oz, said, *"What's his name? Gregory Glaude? His name's not on the list. Sorry he can't go in."* And just like that here was a two-hour drive and all the hype of preparation down the drain. Pastor had not called the prison chaplain to put my name on the list for entry into the prison. It was truly with a heavy heart of disappointment that we turned around and went back to the car. Pastor didn't even seem surprised. It was just matter of fact. *"Oh well. I guess we'll go home then. There's nothing we can do."* It may have seemed okay with the pastor to drive all that way for nothing but to me, I was devastated. I really wanted to go to the prison. I really wanted to meet the men. So why wasn't it happening? Why didn't we get in? Was I not prepared enough? Was I truly ready to meet these men? What did I do? Was it me? I was asking all these questions on the way home and wondering.

About two months later, Pastor JJ, called me again on a Wednesday, I believe, and said, *"We are going to the prison this Sabbath. Do you want to go?"*

"Yes! Of course. But please, can you call the prison and find out if my name is on the list? I don't want to drive out there only to find that my name isn't on the list." Pastor assured me that everything was fine. I know he probably did not call and that he was just trusting that the chaplain had included me.

So, the first time pastor and I went to the prison it was about a two and a half-hour drive. Now this day, we took the church bus with five other people and it was a *"Slow Ride"* to the prison. We left at 4:00 PM in the afternoon and got there at 7:30 PM. When we got to the front desk I was nervous because the same lady was there and it looked like her expression never changed from the last time we were there. She was grim and unhappy to be alive. Fortunately, all of our names were on the list and we proceeded to go through the sign in process. Everyone passed through the metal detector and no one sounded the alarm. And now, the pat-down. They were very serious about bringing absolutely nothing in there that could be misused as a weapon of any type. Then we got our hands stamped with invisible glow-in-the-dark ink...and don't let it wear off or you might not get out! And then we waited for a few more minutes because security had to come and walk us through the prison to get to where we were having church service. I had never been in a prison before. So this is what it's really like. Hmmm. Nope, I don't want to go to prison...other than to visit.

Sssshhhhhhhhhhhhhh. The hydraulic door opened to the side of the room and security called us in. We stopped by this big glass window and showed our hand stamp against this little black light to let them know we've been stamped. Sssshhhhhhhhhhhhhhh and the door closed behind us. Can't get out now! Sssshhhhhhhhhhhhhhh and the door opened in front of us and down the hall we went deeper into the prison. And another door opened and closed with that same hydraulic assurance that no one got in or out unless they let you. There were guard stations along the way. They all seemed fairly friendly. Sssshhhhhhhhhhhhh and now the last door opened to another small hallway and now we entered into the gymnasium. There were chairs and a podium set up, but no one was there. We all kind of stood around for about five minutes or so. All of a sudden, the door to the gym opened and all I heard was, *"Happy Sabbath, brother!" "Happy Sabbath!"* Then I heard the thud of hands shaking very hard! It was indeed a tough guy's hand shake. Men were pouring into the gym and they came to us and greeted us like long lost brothers and sisters. They came to me one by one, *"Happy Sabbath, Brother Greg! So glad you could make it! Can't wait to hear you preach today, brother!"* I was amazed at how friendly and brotherly these men were. They did not seem like criminals at all. In fact, I forgot quickly that I was among such men. They reminded me of Paul in the Bible. These men had done wrong but their lives were changed and I could see that.

The men quickly filled the gymnasium and we were surrounded by the men, the prisoners, most of whom were locked up for life. Somehow, I didn't see them that way. As the men gathered around we all sat as the service began. One by one, different brothers would come up and share a portion of the service. Finally, the Head Elder Martin, came up. This brother was a bit intimidating as his stature was tall and he spoke boldly before the men. I will never forget the words he said after coming forward as long as I live. *"Good evening and welcome to Mountain View of Calvary SDA Church, brothers and sisters. My name is Martin F. S_ _ _ _. I've been in prison for over thirty years and I hope to get out one day, but if I don't, I know who my Lord and Savior is, Jesus Christ. Amen? Amen."* Martin's words resonated in my heart, but more importantly, I felt very intimidated by his words! How was I going to follow that!? What could I say to the men that would inspire them more than what they just heard. All during the service I was listening to the men sing with all their hearts and praising God and there waiting to share a word of encouragement with them. Who was I? I thought, that these men would listen to me? Then, Pastor JJ went up in front of the men and gave me a rousing introduction. Pastor told them that I had a powerful testimony and he wanted them to pay attention to what I had to say. And then Pastor Moses called me up to the pulpit.

So I walked up in front of the men and I placed my Bible and my twelve-page sermon down on the podium and I looked out into the group of about fifty to sixty men and I paused…and then said these words; *"Good evening gentlemen."*

"Good evening, Brother Greg!"

"I want you to know, I have NEVER been in a prison before. This is my very first time. I had no idea of what it was like or what to expect. I want you to know one thing though, I thank God that I will be in Heaven with all you brothers here this evening." And with that, all the men stood up and applauded and thanked me. *"I want you to know that I wrote a twelve-page sermon, which I have right here. But if you don't mind, I'm just going to speak from my heart if that's okay with you."*

"Go 'head, brother! Preach!" And from that moment on, I let the Holy Spirit lead and direct everything I said. I covered the main points I wanted to in my written sermon but I believe the men not only *"Believed"* what I said they also related to what I said. I shared my testimony of drug, alcohol and cigarette addiction. I shared my testimony of the accidents I had been in. And when I was done the men stood up and applauded my sermon and I never felt more close to any church members in my life! However, I never realized it until the very end when we were leaving. A brother called me over to him and said, *"Brother Greg, I have something I want to tell you."*

"What's that?"

"I was a regular at the Classics Night Club and I was there the night of your accident. I'm so happy to see that you're okay and that you came to visit us brother! God bless you, brother!" I was amazed! Only one other time in my life had I met someone with a story about the night of my accident and now two hours away at a maximum security prison, of all places, do I run into a brother who witnessed the nightmare I had been in. Only God could make such an arrangement and meeting. It was NOT fate. This was Divine Destiny at work and God showed His Power and Mercy on us both to allow us this moment of fellowship.

It was now about 10:30 PM as we were leaving the prison doors and I was on such a high from the entire experience of meeting the men! This is what it's like to do Prison Ministry! WOWW! As we drove the three- to four-hour drive back home, I was so pumped up and excited about my experience there that I could not even think of falling asleep on the way home. I wanted to know when we would come back. *"So when will we get to come back Pastor?"*

"We'll see. You did good there. The brothers liked your sermon."

"I too enjoyed the service and everything." So for the next few hours, I just kept reflecting on the highlights of the service. However, one thing kept ringing in my mind… Elder Martin's testimony. I could not get his words out of my head. *"Good evening, brothers and sisters. My name is Martin _ _ _ _ _. I've been in prison for over thirty years and I hope to get out one day, but if I don't, I know who my Lord and Savior is, Jesus Christ. Amen? Amen."* How is that possible? That's a great love for Jesus!

It was several weeks before we would return to the prison. However, I was determined to get even closer to the men. So rather than wear my three-piece suit to the prison, I thought that I would come to church as they did, in jeans, blue shirt, and work boots. That was their dress and attire for worship service. That's all they had and that was all that was needed. So the next time we visited, it was another group of about five to seven of us and I was excited to see them. Again Pastor JJ Moses introduced me and when I came up I asked them if they minded me dressing like them and asked if I could become an *"official member of the Mountain View of Calvary SDA Church"* to which they applauded and welcomed me as a member of their church! They were happy to receive me. They saw that I really cared about them and truly wanted to fellowship and experience them as brothers. And that's it... I have never seen them as prisoners, only Brothers in Christ Jesus. I am in need of just as much forgiveness as they are, maybe more. Pastor JJ saw that I was connecting very well with the men and saw he could trust me with them.

CHAPTER 38

PRISON MINISTRIES: LOCKDOWN

In September of 2013 the prison went on *"lockdown."* This means no visitation whatsoever. By this time, I had the chaplain's email, Chaplain Kevin, and every week I would email him to check on the men and see how they were doing and to find out if the lockdown had been lifted. For six months the prison had been on lockdown, but faithfully, every week I checked on the men. I couldn't wait to get back in the prison to see my brothers and be in their presence. If you have never been to a prison to visit our brothers, I encourage you to find a way to get connected to a Prison Ministry. It was the most powerful experience of ministering I have ever had since I was baptized.

In April of 2014, Chaplain Kevin informed me that we could resume the visitations. However, when I mentioned to Pastor JJ that the prison was coming off of lock-down, he mentioned that I should go in his place and be his representative in his absence. So I went. I made, what was a three-to-four-hour drive, in two hours. And my first solo visit was a huge success. First of all, we had a 11:45 AM service that went to 1:15 PM and I got back home in a much more reasonable time, around 4:30 PM and still had the rest of the day to still do things if needed. But now that I was on my own, I could dictate when and how often I went to the prison. All I had to do was inform the chaplain when I wanted to visit. As it turned out, the third Sabbath or Saturdays of the month were the best days for me to arrange my regular visitations. And this began my Prison Ministry, which I am still doing today. One thing I found out with our brothers in prison is that they count on *"consistency."* If you're thinking about getting involved in Prison Ministry, consider how much and often you will be able to visit and *"Commit to it!"* The worst thing you can do is, *"Do it once just to see what it's like."* The men are looking to build *"relationships"* just like Jesus is looking to build with you and me. I am committed to visiting at least once a month and the reward is really all mine. You cannot imagine how many times I have sat in the prison parking lot just thinking about the brothers I just left and the powerful experience I had with worshipping with these wonderful brothers. While the guards may think otherwise, and have said so, I know these brothers are going to Heaven and will see Jesus Christ in all His glory.

After a while, I noticed that the men did not have Sabbath School Quarterlies, our weekly Bible Study Booklets. So I went to the bookstore and purchased as many as I could and distributed to the men at my next visit. After the services were done, a brother came and whispered in my ear and said, *"Brother Greg, I want to thank you again for loving us so much to continue coming to visit us here. I have to tell you, though; if I hadn't been locked up I may have never given my life to Christ. That's the truth."*

"Praise God that we don't have much longer to wait brother. Be at peace...not much longer now." The fact is, others may see *"Hardened Criminals,"* but I see *"Converted Souls for Jesus Christ."* And that's all that matters. Amen! What a powerful testimony that's TRUE! As I have said many times to these brothers, we must keep pressing on, especially since God has a calling and a purpose for us all.

Today, I am still visiting the North Branch Correctional Institution in Cumberland, MD where we enjoy worship service once a month, usually on the third Sabbath of the month. I have had several partners who joined me in the mission work there including:

my wife, Minerva, Brother Paul, Sister Josephina, Pastor Moses, Brother William, Elder Rob, and now Pastor Pedro who continue to visit with me on a regular basis. Some have left the ministry as sometimes life requires, but I have continued on until this day, with God's blessings. As a friend of mine would say, *"There's always room for more!"* One thing I have learned from the Prison Ministry is that *"God is always willing to forgive ANY sin we've committed."* As long as we confess with our mouth the sin in our hearts that caused me to transgress God's Law of Love, either in thought or deed, then God is *"faithful to forgive us and remember our sins no more."* That's it. I have stated before that I have met *"hardened criminals"* that our judicial system has locked up forever, looked them in their faces and have embraced nothing less than the Love of God and Jesus Christ in their hearts. They may not get a reprieve in this life. They may NEVER be released back into society as we know it. But I know they have already received a *"Full Pardon from Jesus!"* AMEN!

In *The Book of Mysteries* by Rabbi Jonathan Cahn, The Roads Of Zion on page 35 says:

The most famous roads in Zion are not named for what they look like or feel like, nor on their condition. Instead, they have names like the Road to Bethlehem, the Damascus Road or the Emmaus Road, and the Jericho Road. So the most famous roads in Zion are named for places. Their names don't come from what they look like but where they take you. Always look at the end of your course, to where it's taking you. And if you're on the right road, don't get discouraged by the terrain. Never give up. Keep pressing forward to your destination. Because it is the end matters most. And your road, and the journey of your life, will not be known by its terrain, but by the place which it brought you.

The Mission: Today, take your eyes off your circumstances, and focus only on your destination. Press on to the good, the highest, and the heavenly.

I see these men pressing on to find their Creator and their Lord and Savior. What about you? Have you given your life to Jesus Christ? Have you discovered the Miracle of Forgiveness and the Miracle of Grace? If not, then discover Him right now who provides the Gift of Salvation FREELY to you at a price that He alone did pay and could pay. You cannot *"earn"* salvation because it is a *"FREE GIFT."* So will you take hold of the most meaningful gift you could ever receive and claim it as your own? By the way, you can't earn it or work for it or do enough good deeds or live a good enough life to go to heaven. And know this also… NO ONE has preceded any of us in getting to heaven. Our loved ones who have died, no matter how young or old, no matter how nice or generous, have gone to heaven and looking down on us. The Bible tells us the TRUTH about Life and Death and what happens to us when we die. And the TRUTH is, that while it may sound nice and make it easier to believe, not everyone just dies and goes to heaven, especially on their own merits or deeds. Christ only and Christ alone is the way, the truth and the life. *"Jesus said to him, "I am the way, the truth, and the life. No one comes to the Father except through Me"* (**John 14:6**). All I can say and I will leave you with this thought regarding the many men and women in prison… There will be many souls who enter the Gates of Heaven who passed through the iron gates of prison bars long before many of those who watched over them. I have never met more sincere souls who want to receive Jesus Christ than my brothers at Mountain Spring SDA Church in Cumberland, MD.

CHAPTER 39

VOLUNTEER CHAPLAIN

The Lord Jesus always knew why He saved my life, though I have questioned it many times. I too know now why my life was spared through so many accidents and tragedies without so much as a broken bone. Again I say to you; If someone told you, "I know a guy who was hit by a car as a pedestrian and the car was travelling 65mph, then had two serious motorcycle accidents, either of which could have been fatal, then was held at gunpoint by three guys who wanted to rob him, and finally developed stage four cancer and had four spinal surgeries…and if that weren't enough, also had a TIA or *"mini stroke."* you would think that this person would be dead. Yet, here I am today, writing this book that you may read and discover the truth about how God spared my life on several occasions that I might *"Testify to the name of Jesus Christ and give a truthful account about what He has done for me."* Besides saving my physical life, He also saved my *"spiritual life"* giving new life to both. And so with great determination and purpose it was my goal to witness and minister to those in need who were sick and injured. I applied to become a Volunteer Chaplain at Laurel Regional Hospital in Laurel, Maryland, now University of Maryland Laurel Medical Center. Unfortunately, as of December 2018, the Mental Health Department on 4A was closed and relocated to another hospital. However, during the several years I volunteered there I met with those suffering with bipolar disorders, drug abuse, rape and abuse, mental disabilities, chemical imbalances, schizophrenia and those who've attempted suicide.

It all started after I put in my application to become a volunteer sometime in the summer of 2011. For several weeks I had gotten no response from my application. Finally, I found out that a friend from high school, Vikkii, was working as a volunteer in the ER, so I asked her what it took to get in. Later I found out that she had written the hospital chaplain and mentioned what a valuable volunteer they would have if they brought me on board. While that may have remained to be seen, it seems like within a couple of days I got an email from Chaplain Ken to come in for the one-day orientation, which I was glad to do. My assignment was to be on call one day a week in the evening on Wednesday nights. Which meant; if anyone from the ER or another part of the hospital called for the chaplain it was my duty to respond. I was excited to accept the call to duty only to be let down by the lack of calls. Two months went by and not one single call.

Finally, the chaplain called me in to meet with him to discuss my duties because of his upcoming vacation. He mentioned that they may call on me more frequently because of his absence, but most of all, I didn't need to worry about going to 4A, the Mental Health Department. So when the chaplain went on vacation, I finally got a call...where else? 4A. It was a mother who requested me to come and visit with her and her daughter who was being admitted. The nurse in 4A knew nothing of the chaplain's note not to visit 4A, etc. and I could not risk not going and disappointing the mother. So I put on my black suit and tie with a white shirt. I wanted to look *"Official."* When I arrived, I checked into the nurses' station and then waited to meet the mother and daughter. Finally, the nurse set us up in a private room where I conducted our meeting. However, because of HIPPA regulations I am in no way permitted to discuss anything of the nature of our conversation. What I can tell you is, that, after meeting with the woman, daughter and the daughter's husband a little later, I immediately saw the tremendous need for a *"full-time chaplain"* for this department. Before I left, another woman requested that I meet with her. I was happy to listen to her and offer her any comfort I could. I saw the suffering in these people's hearts and I knew now that the Lord had appointed me to serve in this place. It was indeed my calling. I never knew just how much of my pain and suffering would come into use than when I was sitting in front of a group of patients, whom I called *"my friends"* since they had the patience to sit with me for an hour or more. I wrote detailed reports of the peoples' issues and why they were there and then forwarded the information to the chaplain for which he was very grateful.

After about two weeks or so, I realized that I could commit to visiting every Tuesday and Thursday from 6:00 PM to 8:00 PM on a regular basis. I confirmed with my wife and she agreed that this was an important and necessary investment of time. As time went on, all the evening nurses got to know me pretty well and would go around the rooms to invite the patients to my meetings and told them how meaningful they were and that they would benefit from the meetings. However, just as with the Prison Ministry, I believe I received more blessings than I gave. But truly the Holy Spirit was in this place with me as I met with the patients. I have seen right in front of my eyes the transformation of souls that were completely broken and destitute change to one of faith and belief in Jesus and His Power to heal them completely.

My structure of the meeting was simple. I would introduce myself; *"Good evening. I'm Chaplain Greg and I'm here to share my testimony with you, to hear your story, and to pray and anoint you for your healing. Is that okay?"* In the many years I served as a volunteer chaplain, I have seen all sorts of individuals suffering with all types of disorders and brokenness. However, a few special cases come to mind. I remember one evening when I was having a group meeting for about six to seven people. There was this one guy who kept getting up and walking out when I started talking about Jesus Christ's death on the Cross and His Resurrection. He was polite though as he came in and out, back and forth; *"I like you, man, but I just can't get with this stuff about Jesus dying and coming back to life! I can't get that brother... I like you, but that's too much for me."*

I was patient with him because I knew he was struggling with his life and the Truth about Jesus Christ. However, he popped in and out of the room so much that he missed the prayer and anointing service. When I came back the next time he was gone. That's the thing about the Mental Health Department there. I might meet someone today and they'd be gone tomorrow. Or I may see them during the course of a week or longer, so I would get to have more interaction with them. However, in the end, I had to make an impact on these people's lives in the first minute or I could lose them. Many people resisted coming to the meetings asking, *"What's this meeting about? What are we here for?"* and the minute I would say, *"It's a spiritual meeting"* some would leave. However, on several occasions, I would ask the people to stay; *"How do you know what it's going to be like when we've never met? You're presuming I'm a bad guy and I'm going to waste your time? Where else do you have to go this evening?"* So often times they would stay and tell me how glad they were that they did stay. Like I said, I would receive more blessings sometimes than I would seem to give.

CHAPTER 40

REAL PHYSICAL AND MIRACULOUS HEALINGS

As I mentioned, part of the ministry I did as a Volunteer Chaplain was prayer and anointing of the sick. Based on what the Bible says in **James 5:13–16 (NKJV),** [13] Is anyone among you suffering? Let him pray. Is anyone cheerful? Let him sing psalms. [14] Is anyone among you sick? Let him call for the elders of the church, and let them pray over him, anointing him with oil in the name of the Lord. [15] And the prayer of faith will save the sick, and the Lord will raise him up. And if he has committed sins, he will be forgiven. [16] *Confess your trespasses to one another, and pray for one another, that you may be healed.* The effective, fervent prayer of a righteous man avails much. So with this in mind I anointed the sick and prayed over them. And it worked! I'm speaking of real, true, honest to God miracle healings!

THE FIRST MIRACLE HEALING

On one occasion, I met with this group and as they were entering the room I noticed the way this woman was walking. I said to her when she was sitting; *"Are you in pain?"*

"Yes."

"Are you having lower back pain?"

"Yes I am. How did you know?"

"Because I've had two spinal surgeries in my lower back so I rec-ognize they symptoms." That's one thing…when you've been sick and see someone else with the same problem, you recognize it eas-ily. We had our group meeting and then as usual, our prayer and anointing service. Everyone loved the smell of my anointing oil. It was frankincense and myrrh. It has a very sweet aroma and it just left people feeling with a sense of peace. Well, that week, my wife had to go out of town on business and would be gone through the weekend. So rather than do nothing all day, I would go and visit my *"friends"* at the hospital. I saw the same woman Friday, Saturday, and Sunday. Now it was Monday, May 7, 2013. I will never forget this meeting. The woman and I were the only ones in the group meeting this evening. So when we sat down she said, *"Chaplain Greg, I have something to tell you!"*

"What's that?"

"I want you to know that my father is a pastor and my husband is a minister in the church. I have been in church all my life and no one has EVER told me to pray the prayer of healing like you did and claim the healing "in advance" and thank God for it as if it's already done."

"REALLY?"

"So I prayed that prayer Friday, Saturday and Sunday and today on May 7 I was completely healed of my two herniated discs that I needed surgery on! Praise the Lord!" So I replied, *"That's amazing! Well give God the Glory for this! He is an Awesome God!"*

She said, *"All my life, May 7 has had a special meaning to me and I never knew why, but now I know, because on today, this May 7,*

2013 the Lord Jesus healed me!" Well I have to tell you how excited I was for her! She was living the testimony of Jesus Christ and His Healing Power! There is no greater builder of faith than to see someone else receive a blessing and know that God and God alone is responsible for the healing. There was no doctor or surgery or any pain pills involved. Just good ol' fashioned prayer and faith in God, through Christ Jesus that saved this woman from her pain and suffering.

Well, I have to tell you, I pulled out my phone and told the woman that she would have to give me a video testimony so that others might hear this Good News about what God has done for her. I was so happy for this women as she was.

You can see Michelle's Testimony on YouTube:
https://www.youtube.com/watch?v=v4p9pGN2q8Y&t=27s

A few days later, I went back and she was still there and had been talking about me to some of the other patients and so when I walked in a young woman walked up to me and smiled and asked if I was the chaplain. To which I replied, *"Yes, I am… May I help you?"* Well the woman who was healed had told this young girl about our visitations and prayer and she told me this girl had never been to church, EVER and had never prayed before. So when we went in the room, the healed woman walked in and she introduced me to the young girl. She told me, *"I want you to know, I've never been to church before and I have never prayed."* And I replied back, *"And I've never met anyone like you before!"* We had an amazing time talking about the Bible and our experiences of how life can bring pain and suffering but also can bring great JOY if you know how to find it. So that evening for the very first time I led this girl in prayer and I could see how the Lord and the Holy Spirit was moving in that place. I knew there was something special going on. She hugged me and told me *"Thank you so much! I feel so different now after that prayer and anointing! I can't wait to see my daughter!"* I told her that she should teach her daughter about

Jesus because He made them both and that she had a responsibility to teach her daughter.

I asked the girl if she was going to be there tomorrow evening and she told me she would be. Well, I've always made a promise to God that if anyone I met didn't have a Bible, I would find the resources and buy them one. I went to the local Bible Book House and bought a Children's Bible for her five-year-old daughter and a Bible for her. It brought her to tears. When she looked at the Children's Bible she told me she felt more comfortable reading that Bible because it was in simple and plain language for a little child...and that was her. We had covered the first part. Prayer. Now I offered her the invitation to come to my church as soon as she got out the hospital. And sure enough, she showed up at church for the very first time in the summer of 2013. What an Amazing Gift God gave me to experience this! I had no idea how awesome for a person's very first visit to church would be and the impact it would have on me. I sent a notice to the church secretary to let the people know we had a new visitor coming and *"Not to blow it!"* So she came with a friend and had her daughter's Bible in hand. She loved the service and said she would be in touch. That was the last time I saw her. But I have hope that she either already has or will receive Jesus Christ as her Lord and Savior before He comes again. Thank you my Lord for that experience.

THE SECOND MIRACLE HEALING

About a year later I was visiting a group of about six to seven people on a Friday, Saturday, Sunday, and now it was Monday evening when I went in. I had been ministering to this group and anointing them for three days in a row and just before I started the group meeting, one guy was balled up in the chair and in tears. I asked him if he was OK and he said that he was in severe pain. Well, when I inquired, it turned out that he had two herniated discs in his lower back and another herniated disc in his neck and complained that the nurses wouldn't give him any pain medication. *"My friend, I can tell you from experience… for this pain you need morphine and only the doctor can prescribe that. But let me check at the front desk to see what we can do for you."* So with that, I went and reported his condition to the nurses. However, they were already familiar with him because he had been complaining of the pain all day and there was nothing they could do. I went back to the room, shut the door and said, *"Okay everyone, I need you to do me a favor. Please, everyone, get up and we are going to lay hands on him and I am going to anoint him and pray over him for his healing."* So…everyone got up, we laid hands on him, I anointed him and then prayed over him. We all then sat back down and I began the meeting. However, there was something strangely powerful already taking place with the man. We all saw him transform right before our eyes from tears of pain to joy! So I asked him, *"Are you okay?"* His exact response was, *"The Lord Jesus is being gentle with me! I've never felt this way before!"* Then as we watched he started rubbing his legs and within two minutes he stood up completely straight and declared that he was completely healed right in front of five other witnesses. Praise God! Amen! People started saying this was a miracle from God and they witnessed it! One woman said *"I've never seen anything like that before!"* and I told her, *"I see it all the time!"* Well, of course you know what happened next… I pulled out my phone and asked everyone to tell what they witnessed and they all claimed this was indeed a miracle from God.

You can see Mark's Testimony on YouTube:
https://www.youtube. com/watch?v=PDnQaHfk90g

I can personally testify to the severe pain that is caused by one herniated disc, much less two. As the guy was leaving the hospital a few days later I asked him to stay in touch with me and let me know how he was doing. After another month of rehab he ended up at a halfway house where he asked me to come and speak to the men. So I did. They weren't so receptive though but, when you're called, you go and plant as many seeds as you can and pray for the best. About six months later I got a phone message from the guy and he sounded disheartened. In his message he told me that he had fallen off the wagon and gotten back to doing drugs and drinking and that he had lost his healing in his spine. I was so sorry for him because his healing was not only, real, it may have stayed with him the rest of his life. But we'll never know. He wasn't expecting me to come and pray over him again either. However, I told him God is a Merciful God and a Loving God and that all he needed to do was repent his sin and confess it and God would forgive him. I never heard back from the guy that received the healing again. I just hope and pray he found God again.

THIRD MIRACLE HEALING

I don't remember the time frame which this happened, but I do remember the event very well. I had just finished listening to a group of about seven people and was just about to do the anointing for healing and have a final pray when this young, African-American girl walked in. We encouraged her to come in for the prayer, but she was quite hesitant and shy. One woman said to her, *"It's okay, he's going to have prayer for us."* As I started to anoint the people when I got to the young girl, she stepped back, and again the woman said to her, *"It's okay, he's just going to anoint you. Is that okay?"* Though she was hesitant, she received the anointing, however, as soon as I anointed her she started shaking and going into convulsions and then fell on the floor!. The same woman said loudly, *"Ohhh my God, that demon in her is coming out of her!"* Someone ran to the nurses desk and informed them and two nurses rushed in. They ordered everyone out of the room. I tried to stay to see if I could assist, but they told me I had to leave. The group met in the kitchen around the corner and I gathered them together to have prayer with them and to pray for the girl. Two days later, when I returned and was at the nurses' station to prepare for the meeting, that same young girl came to me smiling and I asked her if she was going to join us for the meeting. The girl replied, *"Yes.*

I would like to come to the meeting." The nurse on duty asked her, *"Are you going to be okay? Are you going to have another episode like the other day?"* The girl replied, *"I don't know. It wasn't me."* I am fully convinced that the young girl was possessed by a demon and it was driven out through the anointing. I have no other conclusion because she exhibited two totally different personalities from the two times I saw her. I just praise God for the miracle.

CHAPTER 41

THE GUY WHO WANTED TO DIE

There are so many stories and blessings that came out of the work I did a as Volunteer Chaplain. I will always remember the people whose lives were changed because of that experience, including and especially mine. There are just a couple of stories I want to share because of the impact they had on me and my life. One guy told me that he was there because he wanted to die because no one in his family loved him. After years in prison from the time he was a teenager, until now, early thirties, his own daughters wanted nothing to do with him. As a result, he said he went out to Rt. 301 (a major highway) and just sat down in the middle of the road and hoped he would get hit by a truck…and now he was here at the hospital. I asked him, *"Do you blame your daughters for the way they feel about you, after all, would you want to be around you? Would you be scarred of you if you were in their shoes? Have they ever seen your life change since you've been in prison?"*

And he answered, *"No…"* So I challenged him. *"My brother, you said that you did this because no one loves you. Well Jesus Christ loves you and so do I. Let's just start there."* His composure changed right there and he said, *"You do?"*

"Yes I do and if you'll let me, I will pray with you that Jesus will forgive your sins and help restore your relationship with your daughters."

I mentioned to the young man, *"Before you try to contact your daughters or their mother I'm going to suggest that you "build your relationship with Jesus" and take some time to get to know Him. As you get to know him then he'll start to repair some of the damage in your life that will help you repair your relationship with your daughters. You restore your relationship with God so that your family can see "a new man!" They want nothing to do with the old, so you must become new. You must become "born again!" and if you do that, then "maybe" you'll have a chance at restoring your relationships with your girls and their mother. What do you say?"* I mean to tell you, with tears running down his face he said he was willing to try anything that would bring him closer to his daughters. Again, I had no idea of the outcome of this young man after he left the hospital. I don't know if he's alive or dead. But I do know is that he had HOPE. And I know this, if a person has HOPE they can do anything.

CHAPTER 42

THE GUY WHO WANTED
TO DIE NO. 2

One evening I met another young Black guy who was at the hospital because he had attempted suicide. When I asked him what happened and why he wanted to take his life he explained. *"Well, last week I was about to start a new job driving across country with this trucking company. It was a six-figure job! I just bought a new truck and I was about to be set."*

"And then what happened?"

"So to celebrate, I went out the night before I was going to start my new job drinking and doing crack… I never made it to my job. I never made it to work. So I lost the job. I lost my truck. I lost everything. So I just wanted to die." So I inquired about the young man's background. I asked him, *"Do you go to church at all?"*

"I used to."

"What happened?"

"I just stopped going."

"You don't believe in Jesus anymore?"

"It's not that... I just got lazy, I guess."

"So let me ask you... You were going to start this new job making all this money...right?"

"Yeah, that's right."

"Let me ask you, brother... How much of your money were you going to return to God? Do you think with all your new income that you would honor God with it? Maybe God did you a favor and prevented you from sinking even further. Do you think?"

"I don't know. Maybe."

"Well, us meeting here today is no coincidence. This is not by chance and maybe God wants to get your attention before you get too far away."

As I prayed over him after anointing him, I told him that God has a purpose for him and that he had to discover what that was. That would be his mission right now. Draw close to the Lord and he will lead your steps.

A few months later after the brother got out, I received a phone call while I was pulling up to my house from work. It was him and boy, did he have good news! *"Chaplain Greg, I wanted to call you and let you know how I am doing! I want you to know that I am reading my Bible everyday now and I have a new job! I really appreciate everything you told me and you were right, God is leading my way."*

"Well, praise God, my friend! I am so happy to hear this good news! AMEN! Tell me, are you busy this weekend?"

"No... Why? What's going on?"

"Well, I have been invited to preach at a friend of mine's church for the very first time and I would love for you to join us."

"Absolutely, just give me the address."

"I'll text it to you." That weekend came and I was standing up front sharing my sermon with the brother and sisters and I saw my friend from the hospital show up and he brought a friend. During the sermon I shared how God had saved my life many times through all sorts of life-changing experiences and even near-death situations, including cancer. Just as I had done in the hospital, I asked everyone if there was anyone who was sick to come up front and let me anoint them for their healing. First two or three people came up, including my friend's guest. He walked up to me and whispered in my ear, *"Brother, I'm so glad I came because I have been hearing voices in my head and they've been telling me to kill myself."* So I told the young man, *"Well don't you worry brother, you're in the right place. You're in the House of God and we're going to cast out these demons that are trying to possess your mind and take your life."* At that moment the pastor and I lined up everyone in the church and we prayed over this young man and everyone there that they may be healed.

Once again, we can see the Power of God at work through Jesus Christ and the Holy Spirit. I am doing nothing but following His Command…anoint the sick and pray over them that they may be healed. It is in the obedience to His Word that gives Power to the spoken word of prayer. And it is in the faith of Jesus Christ that empowers us to do His will and be drawn to Him.

The fact is, so many of our encounters in life involve people who come and go. Some come into our lives for but a brief moment and others come for a lifetime. Some only need seconds to minutes to be influenced by us. The question is, *"What influence will you leave on others? What mark will you leave on or in their lives? Will it take seconds or will it take a lifetime to make the mark?"* I don't know, but I am going to keep planting seeds and one day when I look back I hope to see nothing but beautiful flowers that grew all along the way.

CHAPTER 43

THE GIRL GOING TO HELL

So many people lives are affected by the things family members say about us. We shape our thoughts about ourselves and their opinions of us as we grow. Some of those opinions can be very harsh and cruel and do very painful and permanent damage. Such was the case with this young girl I met one evening in my group session. There were about seven or eight people. I don't remember what the others said, but I will never forget and vividly remember her first words to me, *"Hi, my name is _____, and I know I am going to hell."* And I asked her, *"Who told you that?"*

"My family."

"Why would they say such a thing? How do they know you're going to hell?"

"Because of choices I have made."

"And? That's it?"

"Yes. My family are all churchgoers so they've always told me "You're going to hell."

"Well, I don't know about your family but I do know this... We're ALL sinners in need of the Grace of God for the forgiveness of our sins. And ANYONE who repents their sins and confesses them

before God will be forgiven. All you have to do is start here right now and I promise you and Jesus promised that you will be with Him in heaven before your family gets there!" The girl just broke down in tears and told me, *"No one has ever told me I'm going to heaven or ever could. I never believed I could go."* So I knew here was the brokenness in her life but I shared this with her. *"Listen. I want to be clear about something, for every type of sin there is there will be someone in heaven who committed the sin. But they get there through "Confession and Repentance." So I need you to understand this. God "Loves the sinner, but hates the sin." So you can't go on sinning, deliberately committing the act of sin in disobedience to God and expect to live in His Kingdom. That's repentance. Repentance is turning away from sin and asking God to help us "Overcome our sinful desires." Let me put it this way, your family needs to repent their sins just as much as you do or they won't enter into God's Kingdom either."* The girl understood that God was not giving her a free pass to keep sinning. But I can tell you, the smile on her face to know that God loves her and accepts her and paid the penalty for her sin debt was incredible. She smiled the whole way through the rest of the meeting. It made my heart fill with JOY to know that she had received this powerful message of Grace and Truth.

CHAPTER 44

THE DRUG ADDICT AND REHAB

One Tuesday evening, I was doing my regular visit to 4A Mental Health when I met this young man who admitted that he was a heroin user and the reason why he was there is because he had overdosed recently. After meeting with him for a while he disclosed to me that on Thursday he was going to a rehab facility in Baltimore but that his girlfriend, who was also a heroin addict, wanted to get together with him Wednesday evening for one last *"blast,"* meaning one last time getting high before rehab. I told him *"If you go with her you will never make it to rehab. If you really want to quit the drugs you have to leave certain people behind, especially other users, even if they're girlfriends."* And then it dawned on me, so I made him an offer, *"If you don't have a ride to the facility, let me know by tomorrow (Wednesday) afternoon, and I will make arrangements to take you."* Well, he was absolutely taken by the fact that I would offer. So I gave him my phone number and just prayed the next day… *"Please call… Please call! Don't go with that girl or you may never get off the drugs."* Sure enough, Wednesday afternoon I got a call from him asking for a ride to the rehab facility in Baltimore, to which, I gladly replied, *"I'll be there at 7:30 AM!"*

So I emailed my supervisor, Sharon, and explained that I would be a little late the next day and she understood and told me, *"No worries. Take your time."* I was excited the next morning when I got up that I couldn't wait to get to the hospital to pick up my friend. As we rode up the highway, I don't remember the conversation but I do remember thanking him for allowing me to take him there. My heart could rest easy knowing that, at least he's going to get a chance at life off of drugs and that he'll get a fresh start. Sometimes that's all people need is a fresh start and just hit the reset button and get a new perspective on life. That's all Jesus Christ wants for us all… Get a new life in Him.

When we arrived at the facility, it wasn't open yet so we sat for a while and he thanked me for taking him there. I couldn't express more happiness knowing that he was going in the right direction. And then the time came and I said a prayer with him and he departed. I didn't know if I would ever see or hear from him again, but I knew that I left him in the Lord's hands.

A week later, I received a call from a number I didn't recognize, but it was local to the area so I answered. It was my friend from rehab! I was so glad to hear from him. Here is what he told me: *"Chaplain Greg, I'm calling you just to touch base and give you an update. Since I've been here I've been eating well and exercising and lifting weights every day and I really feel good about myself! Thank you so much for bringing me here. I know that if I went with my girlfriend I would have never made it here. So thanks again. It really meant a lot for you to go out of your way for me. No one's ever done that."* Well, those words were like a pot of gold to me. It was worth every second I spent with him and every drop of gasoline I used to get him there. After that call, I never heard from him again. It's been a couple of years now but I trust that our God, our Jesus, our Lord and Savior has taken good care of him and we'll see each other again when Jesus comes. We may not always get to see the *"Fruit on the vine…"* but sometimes, just sometimes we may get a glimpse of the bulbs. That's enough for me.

CHAPTER 45

SPINAL SURGERY NO. 4

Boy, a lot's happened to get me here. I went through some periods of unemployment and did everything I could to earn my income. I did several months working with SEARS Home Improvement selling HVAC and ACs until it became unprofitable for me driving from one end of the state to another with no sales and no income. So in August of 2018 I went back to my sure and solid, UBER driving. For what it's worth, it is indeed a hustle and you have to stay out on the road for hours but you can earn some income, which is better than nothing at all. One day I was driving on Rt. 95 South about forty-five minutes from home when I got the most excruciating pain in my back. I'm telling you, it was the pain of old, the kind of pain that didn't just go away! It was a *"herniated disc"* type pain and I could not deal! I sat and squirmed and moved around until I could find that right position while I was driving. I came home and once I was out of the can the pain subsided, somewhat. This went on for several months and finally, I went to my orthopedic doctor, Dr. Navin, who had already done two spinal surgeries on me.

After explaining the radiating pain I had from my back to around the side of my chest, he did an epidural shot to see if that would relieve the pain. However, the very next day, the pain resumed and I was at its mercy. There is something about pain that makes you, or at least me, say, *"Okay! That's it. Let's do the surgery and get this over with! I don't want any more shots or pills! Let's just go in there and remove the problem so I can get back to life. Period."* In January 2019, we scheduled the surgery for February 4, 2019. However, this was not going to be like the other surgeries where I went in and came out that afternoon. This surgery was much more serious because it was in my middle spinal area and that is much more difficult to operate on because of the lungs and other tissue involved. However, I didn't care about the danger, I just cared about getting rid of the pain.

On February 4, they wheeled me in the OR and when I came out, even though I was in a lot of *"surgical"* pain, I knew that it was a success. However, the road to recover was going to be a bit longer than other surgeries. I can thank my dear, lovely wife, Minerva and dear friend Beasley, for taking good care of me during recovery. I am fully recovered today and I thank God every day for His wonderful Healing Power!

CHAPTER 46

TIA: THE MINI STROKE

Since the beginning of 2019, I had been unemployed because of the herniated discs and surgery that I had to have and by April of 2019 the pressure of earning an income started becoming too much for me. While taking a shower, I was thinking about all the bills and other family issues going on and then I noticed my arm had gone numb…it felt like I had no control over it. I knew something was wrong. It really felt strange. I came out of the shower and dried myself off. Thankfully my wife was working from home that day. When I came in the room I said to her, *"Honey, please pray for me. Something is wrong."* Well, she knew right away that I needed to get to the hospital and wanted to call 911, but I told her to help me get dressed and take me because it would be faster.

PLEASE NOTE

Friends, if you or a loved one, has an episode *"TAKE THIS SERIOUSLY AND REACT IMMEDIATELY!" DON'T PLAY THIS OFF BUT TAKE IMMEDIATE ACTION!"*

Please know that the fact that my wife got me to the Hospital Emergency Room within fifteen minutes of the initial episode the hospital was able to do an immediate MRI on me and give me medications to get me back to normal. Thankfully, I did not suffer a stroke, but what they call a TIA, a Transient Ischemic Attack, known as a mini stroke, which can last for about five to fifteen minutes or so, not very long at all. However, take every health situation seriously. Fortunately for me, they found absolutely no evidence of a stroke or other serious episodes. The doctors kept me overnight for observation and released me. I have been fine ever since. They have me on a regimen of meds to keep it in check and I take my meds regularly.

CHAPTER 47

WHAT I HAVE LEARNED

One thing I have learned throughout my life is to enjoy life as best you can and serve God and people with all your heart, all your soul and all your being and do everything to the very best of my abilities. One this is for certain, the devil himself cannot kill you until it's your time to go. I have seen this repeatedly in my life and the lives of others who have tried to commit suicide. This does not mean you *"tempt"* God or try Him. I know for a fact that my life could have easily been taken during any of the incidents I described without question and yet God said, *"Not yet."* I never knew the plans God had in store for me, but He did. I didn't see myself doing Prison Ministry, but He did. I didn't see myself ministering to hundreds of people in the Mental Health Department at UMD Laurel Regional Hospital, but He did. I didn't see myself writing this book and sharing all this information about what God has done for me through Jesus Christ, our Lord and our Savior, but He did. Don't let the bumps in the road stop you or even slow you down. Do what God has called us all to do and that is *"Testify of His Good Name and tell people what Jesus Christ and the Holy Spirit have done for you!"*

TIMES MY LIFE WAS SPARED

ACCIDENT #1 CAR ACCIDENT: Most certainly, on March 12, 1983, my life was not only spared but even after being hit by a car travelling 65mph and thrown approximately 40-50 yards down the road and rolling over and over on the asphalt, I did not get a broken bone. I believe sincerely, with all my heart, that my guardian angel wrapped me in his wings just before the accident and rolled with me until I came to a stop in the middle of Allentown Road in Camp Springs, MD. I can only conclude that in the process of changing the course of my life permanently and completely God showed me His mercy and love by letting me experience something that I know had to have been a miracle. He put His stamp on this so that I would know. Everyone who has heard this testimony cannot deny God's intervention. No one gets hit by a car travelling 65mph and doesn't get a bone broken. That just doesn't happen. It's not *"karma or fate"* it was *"GOD"* and He alone spared me. Please know that I believe if I had a conversation with God about this it may have sounded like this: *"My son, I love you dearly, but you were making plans that I could not endorse. You could not see yourself doing the things that I have called you to do. You didn't see yourself doing the ministries that I had in store for you, but I did. So as painful as this will be, I will let you know that I am with you always and will never leave you nor forsake you. One day you will know, and you will recognize this in a very special way."* I have never asked God, *"Why?"*

ACCIDENT #2 MOTORCYCLE ACCIDENT 1: The second time that I recall my life being spared was during a motorcycle accident that happened four blocks from home. It was a nice hot summer day and I did not have on my leather jacket and gear as I normally would. I was just cruising along heading home when a car pulled out in front of me crossing the road. I immediately hit my horns, which were after-market truck horns, so I knew the person could hear me, but he kept rolling slowly out in front of me until finally I just slammed on my breaks and I went into a slide…heading right towards the vehicle. Your life really does flash before you! I saw myself heading right towards the car and I braced myself thinking I was going to slam right into this vehicle. But as accidents happen, sometimes there are no explanations for what happened next. Somehow, I went around the *"front of the car"* and ended up in the turning lane on the opposite side of the island. Scientifically…this was physically impossible! I should have ended up under this vehicle or at least a splat on his driver's side passenger door. But no, I went around this vehicle, while we were both still moving and there is but one explanation that makes sense. God. God and only God could have intervened. God sent my guardian angel to do what he does best, which is *"guarding my life"* and he executed his assignment and did what he was supposed to do…save my life…again. I owe him a lot by now. Let me explain. See the diagram.

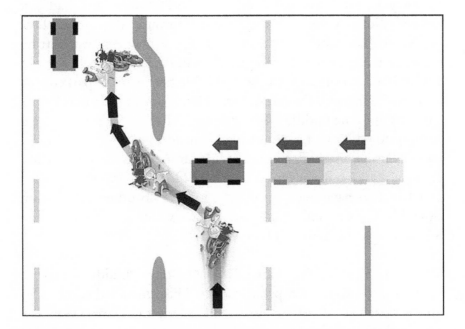

As you can see, I was travelling straight down the road when the car came out from the right-side parking lot and when I hit my horns he just kept coming. I didn't know if he was going to stop and let me pass or keep coming because he really did not see me. Physics say with the speed I was travelling, about 45-50mph, once the bike started sliding it keeps going in the direction of the slide, straight…right into the vehicle. So then…how do I end up on the opposite side of traffic, in the island area for cars turning into the parking lot? Well, I've given you my answer, but you can believe what you want. I have to just share the facts. The fact is, the guy kept on going after seeing me laying in the street and I walked my motorcycle home with just a road rash and some bruises, again, without a broken bone.

ACIDENT #3 MOTORCYCLE ACCIDENT 2: I must really have nine lives like a cat or something because I kept having these accidents in which my life was not only spared but surviving without a broken bone. I'm not complaining at all. I was riding my motorcycle, my Ninja ZX7, on New York Avenue and had just crossed North Capital Street headed towards downtown DC. Traffic was heavy but normal for 1pm on a Friday. As I was getting closer to the next intersection traffic had backed up so, being me, I went between the cars on the right side between the parked cars and moving cars on the left of me. When I got to the intersection, I was right in the middle when, BAAAAMMM!! I got hit by a car turning to go down the side street. I mean I got *"T-Boned"* and I went over the hood of the car, the bike dropped to the ground and I, amazingly, landed on my feet! Only God! Again, my guardian angel had to have been on duty! There is no other explanation how this happens and again I walked away without a scratch! Just a busted ego and a broken bike.

While I was getting the woman's information my buddy, Tom, who happened to drive a dumpster truck had just unloaded and had an empty bed. Talk about having friends at the right time. Tom saw me on the side of road, went one block down and dropped that two-ton bed in the middle of the street and let me roll the bike on the back and gave me a ride to his house. As they say, *"You just can't make this stuff up!"*

INCIDENT #4: The Hallway Robbery Attempt. Here is another example of God's love for me because this was still years before I had given my life to the Lord, Jesus. I won't bore you with the details again but let me say this. Once again, I believe with absolute certainty that God spared my life by sending my guardian angel once again because this was too, too bizarre. During the abduction, when they pulled me out of my door and walked me to the elevator, the guy with the gun turned his back to me. I got it in my head, *"Don't get shot."* So I lunged over his shoulders and grabbed the gun with both my hands and locked my hands preventing him from turning around and shooting me. I started screaming to my neighbors to call the police, they have a gun and they are trying to shoot me. The other two guys ran, one left the building. During this altercation, we fell against the wall, slid down the wall and I still managed to keep my hands locked on the gun. Two words… FEAR and ADRENALIN. However, there was a point when we were past F&A and we're now back to physics. One of the guys, the biggest one, came back and punched me in my head and kicked me in my spine. The guy I was wrestling with slid the gun across the floor so the big guy could grab it. HOWEVER, I managed to grab less than half an inch of the gun's handle and this guy, who was standing over me and had *"leverage"* could not take the gun away! Physics says, *"**He should have easily been able to take the gun out of my hand.**"* But God said, *"No, not yet. It's not your time."* Somehow, both me and the guy who had the gun managed to stand back up in the same position with me locking hands around his and the gun until the gun fired in the hallway. The big guy backed off, ran down the hall and the guy with the gun wrestled it away from me and ran after his friends. And yes, I will say it again, I believe with all my heart, mind and soul that my guardian angel was there again to keep me from getting shot and/or killed that night. I don't know about you, but I am giving my guardian angel a real work out here. He's going to have a lot of extra medals and awards for all the work I've been giving him. I can't wait to thank him for serving the Lord, Jesus Christ as he has to spare my life so many times. It's not easy being an angel. They have endured some real battles, just read the Bible. They're in there. Thank you.

CHAPTER 48

FINAL NOTE

TRIALS. TRIUMPH & THE VICTORY IN A NUTSHELL.

<u>TRIALS:</u> These are the things that happen to everyone daily and depending on the situation, some days can be more trying than others. If you have not experienced any trials in your life, you either aren't living or it isn't your turn yet, but you will. As a dear friend of mine used to say, "You've got some dues to pay." Just know that God uses every trial we face to *"Draw us near to Him"* that we may know Him better. It is the trials that put us on our knees in prayer to Him to give us relief and strength to get us through them. Just know that God will not end a trial for the sake of our comfort but will allow them to continue as He molds our character more like His. The Bible says this about "trials".

<u>James 1:2–4 NKJV</u> **Profiting from Trials** *"My brethren, count it all joy when you fall into various trials, knowing that the testing of your faith produces patience. But let patience have its perfect work, that you may be perfect and complete, lacking nothing."*

<u>TRIUMPH:</u> We are not responsible for this part. Jesus gives us His Triumph that He won when He died on the Cross of Calvary for our sins. We can only have true triumph by accepting His *"Free Gift"* of Salvation. We experience triumph when we confess our

sins to Him and are released from the burden and guilt that sin brings. The Bible says this about "triumph".

Psalm 41:11 NKJV *"By this I know that You are well pleased with me, because my enemy does not triumph over me."*

Psalm 47:1 NKJV *"Oh, clap your hands, all you peoples! Shout to God with the voice of triumph!"*

Romans 5:1 NKJV Faith Triumphs in Trouble *"Therefore, having been justified by faith, we have peace with God through our Lord Jesus Christ;."*

VICTORY: The Victory in Christ is ours after we receive the Holy Spirit. As we share the Good News of what He has done for us we experience the victory here and now. When Jesus Christ comes again to take us all home to Heaven. The victory also comes as we overcome sin and beat Satan at his game who wants to cause us to lose Salvation. Nothing this world has to offer is worth losing the victory we have in Jesus Christ. The Bible says this about "victory".

1 Corinthians 15:57 NKJV *"But thanks be to God, who gives us the victory through our Lord Jesus Christ."*

1 Peter 1:6–7 NKJV *"In this you greatly rejoice, though now for a little while, if need be, you have been grieved by various trials, ⁷ that the genuineness of your faith, being much more precious than gold that perishes, though it is tested by fire, may be found to praise, honor, and glory at the revelation of Jesus Christ,"*

1 John 5:4 NKJV *"For whatever is born of God overcomes the world. And this is the victory that has overcome the world—our faith."*

MISSION: Take your Trials and turn them into Triumphs for Christ and receive the Victory of Jesus Christ through the Holy Spirit and do something that will have "Eternal Value". Tell people what Jesus Christ has done for you **AND LIVE!**

Prayer, surrendering to Christ and repentance of sin are the most powerful thing any of us can do for ourselves and for others. I have had the pleasure of ministering to people in the hospital and have seen the power of prayer work real miracles of healing in peoples' lives. Here are two links for testimonies that I posted of friends I met in the hospital who both had herniated discs in their spines and were healed through prayer and anointing the way that James 5:13-16 says to do in the Scriptures.

Michelle's Testimony: https://m.youtube.com/watch?v=v4p-9pGN2q8Y

Mark's Testimony: https://m.youtube.com/watch?v=PDnQaHfk-90g&t=1s

Lastly, to all those who have read this book I want you to know that my brother and I have been clean for many years now and desire to serve as best we can our fellow neighbors daily.

Gregory Austin Glaude, clean for over twenty years now. A graphic designer with his freelance business, Brainstorm Graffix. Serves as Lead Volunteer at. N.B.C.I. (North Branch Correctional Institution) in Cumberland, MD. Former Volunteer Chaplain at MDU Laurel Regional Hospital worked with mental health patients in recovery.

Stephen Anthony Glaudé (brother), clean for over twelve years now. Currently, CEO of CNHED the (Coalition for Nonprofit Housing and Economic Development) where he is helping many of the residents of Washington, DC with housing and other issues and serving his community and doing what he does best, community service and leading others to do their very best each day.

Many of the people who were connected to Greg's drug addiction, including other addicts and drug dealers have reformed and have cleaned their lives up and are doing extremely well. You all should know that if someone you love is going through any type of addiction or illness, NEVER GIVE UP and ALWAYS PRAY. Our stories don't end until we are dead. As long as there is breath in us keep your faith in Jesus Christ, our Lord and our Savior. Finally remember this…

"Let your conduct be without covetousness; be content with such things as you have." For He Himself has said, "I will never leave you nor forsake you." (Hebrews 13:5)

THE END

Please note: All the Bible verses quoted in this book are from the New King James NKJV version.

Gregory with his sister Kristina Smith and brother, Stephen Glaudé

Love Always & All ways, Gregory & Minerva Glaude

REFERENCES

My personal life experiences, by Gregory Austin Glaude

The Spirit Filled Life Bible NKJV, Published by: Thomas Nelson Publishers

The Book of Mysteries, by Jonathan Cahn, Published by: Front Line

ABOUT THE AUTHOR

Gregory Austin Glaude was born Saturday, November 1, 1958, in Washington, DC, at Washington Hospital Center to his parents, William Criss and Phyllis Taylor Glaude, older sister, Kristina and older brother Stephen. From the early age of two years old, his mother said she knew he was going to be an artist. He loved to draw and paint, and it was in his senior year of high school that he endeavored to take art classes and take up art studies in college. During his early teen years, he experimented with drugs, such as marijuana and beer and alcohol. Later, he started using barbiturates (speed) cocaine and finally crack cocaine.

In 1997, Gregory became a *"born-again Christian"* in the Seventh-Day Adventist Church while still battling his addictions until finally he fully surrendered them to Jesus Christ, our Lord. After giving up all his addictions in year 2000, he overcame them all through prayer and Bible studies. He never once attended a rehab facility or used other drugs to overcome his addictions.

Subsequently, in 2006, Gregory was diagnosed with a stage four cancerous tumor in the base of his tongue. He endured thirty radiation treatments, eight chemotherapy treatments, and finally, four days of brachytherapy treatment, having his mouth wired shut, a trachea tube inserted in his throat, and eighteen catheters sewn in his chin as the final phase of his treatment. In 2008, Gregory's cancer returned and did not receive a good prognosis or good chance of survival from his doctors at NIH (National Institutes of Health). After two months of testing, his close friends, Gary and Linda and family, anointed him and prayed over him and he claimed the healing. Prior to a biopsy procedure a few days later, Gregory told his doctors, *"Don't be surprised. My wife and I have prayed about this and God has healed me."* One doctor replied,

"I'm glad you're thinking positive." He replied, *"No, it's not positive thinking. God has healed me."* They went in to do the procedure and after one hundred samples taken with a pathologist in the operating room, they could not find the cancer and he is still healed to this day. In thanksgiving to our Lord and Savior, Jesus Christ, Gregory works daily to share the message of the Gospel and what the Lord has done for him. If you want him to visit your church or come as a motivational speaker, feel free to contact him at: gregoryglaude358@gmail.com.

Since then, Gregory and his wife, Minerva, have been doing a prayer ministry and are on call for anyone who needs prayer for healing. They have anointed several people who have been sick and many of them have made a full recovery. One person was actually healed of two herniated discs in his spine in the presence of six other witnesses. Additionally, Gregory has served as a volunteer chaplain at UMD Laurel Regional Hospital working with mental health patients in the Mental Health Department (now closed) and also visits the maximum security prison in Cumberland, MD once a month to have worship services with over sixty men in their Adventist congregation until COVID19. Gregory hopes the prison will open up soon and be able to resume his visits with his brothers in the prison.

Finally, Gregory hopes that the publication of his testimonies will help others who are struggling with addiction/s and/or faith issues and questions. We are all on the same planet breathing the same air struggling with the same struggles. Let us love and care for one another until Jesus comes again. Amen.